*T*his book
belongs to

_____

…*a woman after God's
own heart.*

GROWTH AND
STUDY GUIDE

A
Woman
After
God's Own
Heart®

ELIZABETH GEORGE

HARVEST HOUSE PUBLISHERS
Eugene, Oregon 97402

Acknowledgment

As always, thank you to my dear husband, Jim George, M.Div., Th.M., for your able assistance, guidance, suggestions, and loving encouragement on this project.

~A Word of Welcome~

Please let me welcome you to this fun—and stretching!—growth and study guide for women like you who want to live out God's priorities. And please let me commend you for taking your journey toward becoming a woman after God's own heart one step further.

A Word of Instruction

The exercises in this study guide should be easy to follow and to work. You'll need your copy of the book *A Woman After God's Own Heart*™[1] and your Bible, a pen, a dictionary, and a heart ready to grow. In each lesson you'll be asked to:

- Read the corresponding chapter from *A Woman After God's Own Heart*™.
- Answer the questions designed to guide you to greater growth.
- Select a verse or two that relate to the exercises to memorize and to hide in your heart.
- Pray about and put into action the priority discussed.
- Write out a 100-word homework assignment.

A Word for Your Group

Of course, you can grow (volumes!) as you work your way, alone, through these truths from God's Word and apply them to your heart and home. But I urge you to share the journey with other women. A group, no matter how small or large, offers personal care and interest. There is sharing. There are sisters-in-Christ to pray for you. There is the mutual exchange of experiences. There is accountability. And, yes, there is peer pressure…which always helps us to get our lessons done! And there is sweet, sweet encouragement as together you stimulate one another to greater love and greater works of love (Hebrews 10:24).

To aid the woman who is guided by God to lead a group, I've included two sections in the back of this growth and study book:

- Instructions on how to lead a group discussion, and
- Discussion questions written for your group

A Word of Encouragement

What is it worth, dear one, to have a heart and a home that honor God and are pleasing in His eyes? Is it worth spending a few minutes a day or a few hours in a week internalizing the principles found in *A Woman After God's Own Heart*™ and in this growth and study guide? What I'm offering you here is the opportunity to take what you're learning to a deeper level and to work it out in your home and family, to live out what you know you want to do and be–a woman after God's own heart.

If you will use the insights, tools, and how-to's gained from the book *A Woman After God's Own Heart*™ and from this study guide, by God's grace and with His help, people who know you will begin to describe *you* as a woman after God's own heart. Your ways will bring glory to Him. It's work. I know that. But it's also joy–the deep joy of knowing God's will and doing God's will. So please, enjoy the journey…for the rest of your life!

Contents

A Word of Welcome

The Practice of God's Priorities

Heart Exercise 1

A Heart Devoted to God

 In your personal copy of *A Woman After God's Own Heart*™[1] read chapter 1, "A Heart Devoted to God." Make notes here about what meant the most to you from this chapter or offered you the greatest challenge or inspired you deeply.

Did you enjoy observing the contrast between the two sisters, Mary and Martha? I know that carefully considering their lives touched mine (in more ways than one!). Read their story in your Bible in Luke 10:38-42. Try to imagine the scene yourself. For instance...

Where did the story take place?

And what was going on?

Who were the people present?

How did Martha act...and why?

And how did Mary act?

What were Jesus' words to Martha?

And His words to Mary?

As I noted on page 13 of the book, Martha was so busy doing things *for* the Lord that she failed to spend time **with** Him. Mary, however, put worship at the top of her to-do list. As a woman after God's own heart, Mary made a choice that indicated *a heart of devotion*. She knew it was important to cease her busyness, stop all activity, and set aside secondary things in order to focus wholly on the Lord. List at least five actions you can take to put worship at the top of your to-do list.

1.

2.

3.

4.

5.

Write out below what you will do daily—just for this next week—to...

...cease your busyness,

...stop all activity, and

...set aside secondary things

in order to focus wholly on the Lord. Then give thought to this quote:

> Modern civilization is so complex as to make the devotional life all but impossible. It wears us out by multiplying distractions and beats us down by destroying our solitude, where otherwise we might drink and renew our strength before going out to face the world again.[2]

Do you have a dictionary nearby? Look up the definition of the word "priority" and write it out as simply as you can here.

Now, purpose to choose God as your first and ultimate priority by having a daily time with Him. I've provided a "Quiet Times Calendar" for you to use each day throughout this study (see pages 148-149). Just fill in the squares for each day that you have a quiet time. Remember that the goal is solid lines like a thermometer—not a "morse code" measurement (dot-dot-dash) or a "measles" measurement (here a dot, there a dot)! I know you'll be blessed, just as the woman who wrote this was:

> I have been attempting to have daily quiet times for awhile now. This past week, however, I found that having to actually record the days I had my quiet time has encouraged me to be more faithful with them. Instead of brushing it aside in the morning, I chose to have it, even if it couldn't be as long as I hoped for.

And while you've got the dictionary out, go ahead and look up the definition of the word "worship" and, again, write it out as simply as you can here.

Now, make a schedule for next week that includes a scheduled "quiet time" with God in His Word and in prayer. (And don't forget—*something is better than nothing! Aim for consistency.* Begin with even a brief time each day. Great lives are made up of many "little" disciplines! Begin the "little" discipline of meeting with the Lord daily and then filling in your Quiet Times Calendar.)

♡ Another help discussed on page 16 was Proverbs 3:6. Read this verse in your Bible and write it out here.

Now, purpose to actively choose God and His ways at every decision, word, moment, thought, and step—today and every day of the week. This is what it means to make God your Ultimate Priority, to walk with Him moment by moment and step by step. Your heart's desire should be to prefer God and His way in all things. Seek to ask God these questions before you speak or act:

What do You want me to say? Lord, what do You want me to do?

♡ Another valuable principle in the "Yes, But How?" section of your book was stated:

Good, better, best,
never let it rest,
until your good is better,
and your better best.

Can you think of any area in your life where you are consciously settling for *good* when you know that a *better* and a *best* choice are available? Make a note of it here...and then set out to make God's better way your way.

Verses to memorize–Luke 10:42 and Proverbs 3:6. Why not hide in your own heart these verses that speak of a heart after God?

 Optional exercise–If you have *A Woman After God's Own Heart™ Prayer Journal*,[3] just for today fill in the section titled "My Relationship with God" by writing out this statement and finishing it with words out of your own heart:

Lord, just for today, help me to cultivate a hot heart by…

On the following page, relate in 100 words or less one instance when you were aware that you actively chose God as a priority over something or someone else this week. Then thank God for that opportunity.

Heart Exercise 2

A Heart Abiding in God's Word

 In your personal copy of *A Woman After God's Own Heart*™ read chapter 2, "A Heart Abiding in God's Word." Make notes here about what meant the most to you from this chapter or what offered you the greatest challenge or inspired you deeply.

"Am I flourishing or failing? Thriving or wilting? Blossoming or withering?" These are questions we would do well to ask ourselves regularly about our spiritual condition. And abiding in God's Word is one sure way to develop a root system that causes us to draw from the Lord all that we need to enjoy a flourishing, thriving, blossoming life. Let's take a few minutes to learn more about roots.

♥ *Roots are unseen*—How is your "underground" life, the time you spend abiding in God's Word and prayer...out of sight, alone, in secret? Before we move on, search your heart and jot down a few honest answers to this all-important question.

What is the first word of Psalm 1, a psalm that spends three verses describing a woman (or man) who is flourishing, thriving, and blooming?

How does the person of Psalm 1 approach the Word of God according to verse 2a?

And what does she do (verse 2b) with what she finds in God's Word?

Note the results listed in verse 3 that come from time spent in God's Word:

Make a schedule for this week that includes a time each day to withdraw from people, projects, and pressures to spend unseen, private time alone with God, nurturing your roots with His Word and communing with Him. And don't forget to say "no" to a few "things."

> We must say "no" not only to things which are wrong and sinful, but to things pleasant, profitable, and good which would hinder and clog our grand duties and our chief work.[4]

♥ *Roots are for taking in*—Consider again my friend Karen and her time of "taking in" on pages 26-27. Are you more like the breathless, frazzled, fretting, and worrying women in that scenario—or are you more like Karen, recognizing the need to slip away for a few minutes alone with the Lord when tensions mount? Write down an honest answer about how you tend to handle the pressures of life. Consider, too, how those closest to you would answer this question about you!

This is a good time to look at Isaiah 58:11 in your Bible. Here God describes the blessings that will be poured out upon those who seek after God in the right ways. List them here:

How can you remember to sink your roots down deeper to take in the "waters [that] do not fail" when life heats up?

Roots are for storage—When I go through tough and trying times, I try to think of every verse of Scripture that I've memorized that can help me through those trials. Do you have a reservoir of verses hidden in your heart? Can you write down two or three that you could (or do) draw upon for strength and endurance? Thank God for these gems from His Word, and don't forget to share them with others when they're in need of "a word in season" (Isaiah 50:4).

Next look at Jeremiah 17:5-8 in your Bible. Verse 8 describes those who hope in and trust in the Lord. Jot down a few of their characteristics.

Then contrast the person who trusts in man versus the person who puts his hope and trust in the Lord.

When we trust in the Lord instead of ourselves, "the contrast in vitality is between being like a parched dwarf juniper in the desert or a tree drawing sustenance from a stream to bear fruit."[5] Are you remembering to turn to God and His Word, to trust in Him, and enjoy the blessings of fruitbearing—even in times of drought?

Roots are for support—Is yours a life marked by the repeated need to be constantly staked up, tied up, propped up, and straightened up, until the next wind comes along and you topple once again? If so, what will you do today to strengthen your root system in the Lord so that you can profit from the power a network of strong roots provides?

A challenge was issued on page 30 to *design a personal time for drawing near to God.* Let's do that now, remembering that...

> The redeemed heart longs
> for communion with God.[6]

First, pick a time—*When* do you think you could be most consistent in having a quiet time each day? Examine your schedule and pick a time. (Don't forget to write it on your schedule!)

Next, pick a place—*Where* do you think you could enjoy the peace and quiet you need for your "quiet" time? (Remember, a door, some privacy, and solitude help!)

And now, pick a plan—*What* tools or aids can make your quiet time most meaningful? Reread the suggestions on page 31 to trigger your own ideas.

And now it's time to dream (see pages 32-33)! Jot down today's date and then describe the woman you desire to be spiritually in one year.

Next describe the woman you desire to be spiritually ten years from now.

Verses to memorize–Why not memorize the verses you selected for your answers in the *Roots are for storage* section? And, if you already know those verses by heart, select several others to memorize.

Optional exercise–If you have *A Woman After God's Own Heart™ Prayer Journal*, just for today fill in the section entitled "My Relationship with God" by writing out this statement and finishing it with words out of your own heart:

Lord, just for today, help me to draw near to You by…

On the following page, relate in 100 words or less one instance when you were aware that you actively chose time in God's Word as a priority over something or someone else this week. Then thank God for that opportunity.

Heart Exercise 3

A Heart Committed to Prayer

In your personal copy of *A Woman After God's Own Heart*™ read chapter 3, "A Heart Committed to Prayer." Make notes here about what meant the most to you from this chapter or offered you the greatest challenge or inspired you deeply.

♡ Of course, Jesus Christ is the Ultimate Example of a Person of prayer. Read Mark 1:35 for a glimpse of Jesus at prayer. What can you learn about His prayer life?

Now describe in a few words what preceded this quiet moment in verses 21-34.

Is your head spinning? Mine is! But Jesus shows us how to handle the "head-spinning" events of busy, hectic, challenging days. How can you follow His example today?

Let's review the seven blessings of prayer listed in this chapter.

Blessing #1: A deeper relationship with God–As you consider that prayer increases faith, provides a place to unload burdens, teaches us that God is always near, trains us not to panic, and changes lives, which one of these benefits would be the greatest reason for developing a heart committed to prayer at this stage of your life? Why?

Blessing #2: Greater purity–I shared with you my problem with gossip in this area of purity. Now won't you identify your particular problem area and share briefly what you plan to do about it?

Blessing #3: Confidence in making decisions–Look again at the picture of Jesus at prayer in Mark 1:35. What was the result of His time in prayer in the area of decision-making (verses 36-39)? What difference did prayer make in the direction for His new day? And what difference might prayer make in the direction for your new days?

Blessing #4: Improved relationships–Hear the words of this wife about an improved relationship!

I committed to the Lord that for this day, which happened to be my husband's day off, I would not argue with him. Recently we had been going through a season that, no matter how hard we tried not to argue, it was happening anyway.

I was praying that my day would be what the Lord willed it to be, and that He would be glorified, yet I had not made a specific commitment to what I could do alone to help the situation, which was part of the problem. The thought of actually committing myself to the Lord, that I would not argue even if my buttons got pushed, seemed different to me. And so I did it.

Well, the situation arose, and I heard the soft voice [of God] reminding me of this commitment. I honored it, and He did too. There was no argument. Praise the Lord!

What relationship do you need to improve through prayer, and how can you begin immediately to commit to pray about that relationship?

Blessing #5: Contentment–Identify an area in your life where you struggle with contentment. Now look at Philippians 4:10-13. What can you learn about contentment from these words from the apostle Paul? How can you apply Paul's lessons to your own situation?

Blessing #6: God-confidence–How do these scriptures increase your trust in God?

Psalm 34:9–

Psalm 84:11–

Blessing #7: The ministry of prayer–Edith Schaeffer stated, "Interceding for other people makes a difference in the history of other people's lives." Who are the people you can minister to through prayer, and when do you plan to begin this "ministry"?

As you look one more time at these seven blessings, realize that these are blessings that you, too, can know as you cultivate a heart of prayer.

Read again the suggestions made on page 44 for cultivating a heart committed to prayer. After writing down which one(s) you will put into practice today, read my own story:

> I know that I do a very unspiritual thing whenever I'm slipping in the discipline of daily prayer. I get out my kitchen timer, set it for five minutes, and pray, "Lord, I'm going to pray just five minutes today." Then, when the timer rings and I've prayed for the full five minutes, I give myself permission to get up from prayer and go on with my day. I don't worry about the fact that my prayer time was only five minutes long. No, I rejoice that I prayed, acknowledging once again that *something is better than nothing!* I rejoice that I've taken the first step toward rebuilding the coveted discipline of prayer.

Verses to memorize—Psalm 46:1; Psalm 121:1-2; Mark 1:35. Choose your favorite from among these verses or pick another verse that encourages your commitment to prayer.

Optional exercise—If you have *A Woman After God's Own Heart*™ *Prayer Journal*, just for today fill in the section titled "My Relationship with God" by writing out this statement and finishing it with words out of your own heart:

Lord, just for today, help me to seek You through prayer by…

On the following page, relate in 100 words or less one instance when you were aware that you actively chose time in prayer as a priority over something or someone else this week.

(And don't forget to pay attention to your Quiet Times Calendar!)

Heart Exercise #4

A Heart That Obeys

 In your personal copy of *A Woman After God's Own Heart*™ read chapter 4, "A Heart That Obeys." Make notes here about what meant the most to you from this chapter or offered you the greatest challenge or inspired you deeply.

💜 It's time to get out your dictionary again. This time look up the word "obedient." To crystalize its meaning in your mind and heart, write the definition out as simply as you can here.

💜 In the section titled "Two Kinds of Hearts," we contrasted the disobedience of King Saul with the obedience of David. Make notes on these instances of Saul's disregard of God's commands through His prophet Samuel:

What specific instructions and promise did Samuel give to Saul in 1 Samuel 10:8?

Seven days later, what happened (see 1 Samuel 13:8-9)?

When Samuel finally arrived and asked Saul, "What have you done?" how did Saul answer in verses 11-12? (Or, put another way, how many excuses did he give and how many different people did he blame?!)

What was Samuel's assessment of Saul's disobedience, and what was the result (verses 13-14)?

For another look at Saul's failure to obey the Lord, look at 1 Samuel 15:1-9. What were Samuel's direct instructions to Saul (verse 3)? (If you think this command sounds harsh, look at Exodus 17:8-16.)

What did Saul do (1 Samuel 15:7-9)?

When Samuel arrived (verse 12) and asked Saul, "What... is this bleating of the sheep in my ears...?" (verse 14), how did Saul answer in verse 15? (Or, put another way, how many excuses did he give and how many different people did he blame this time?!)

Again, what was Samuel's assessment of Saul's disobedience, and what was the result (verses 21-23)?

This growth and study guide is all about becoming a woman after God's own heart. As we considered David, who was a man after God's own heart (Acts 13:22), we noted that David was willing to obey God, lived to serve God, was concerned with following God's will, was centered on God, exhibited a heart after God over the long haul, and humbly depended upon God (page 49).

The fact that you are reading this book and doing this study indicates your desire for a heart that obeys. So...it's time for some honest personal application and heart searching! Can you think of any situations in your life where you are making excuses about your disobedience? Or blaming someone else for your disobedience? Or obeying God only halfway? As I wrote on page 48, "The heart God delights in is a heart that is compliant, cooperative, and responsive to Him and His commands, a heart that obeys." Obedience is a heart issue, so take the time to examine your life, your relationships, your marriage, and your conduct for areas of willful disobedience or half-hearted obedience.

Write out a personal prayer of commitment to make yours a walk in obedience. You may want to use a piece of paper. Then set about to take the step below:

> The most difficult part of obeying God's laws
> is simply deciding to start now.[7]

Here's a list of several proven guidelines from pages 51-54 that can help us to walk in obedience.

Concentrate on doing what is right–What warning does James 4:17 give?

Cease doing what is wrong–What is the instruction of Proverbs 16:17?

Confess any wrong–What does 1 John 1:8-9 teach us?

Clear up things with others–What does Matthew 5:23-24 exhort?

Continue on as soon as possible–What principles do Philippians 3:13-14 give us?

These questions from the "Heart Actions" section of your book bear repeating here:

–Read 1 Peter 2:1 and begin a list of heart attitudes and behaviors that hinder growing a heart of obedience. Which, if any, are hindering the growth of your heart?

–Read Ephesians 4:25-32 and Colossians 3:5-9 and then add to your list those actions and attitudes which need pruning. Again, what do you need to prune from your heart? Be specific.

–Now focus on the positive and consider cultivating what is necessary for growth. Read 1 Peter 2:2, Ephesians 4:15-32, and Colossians 3:1-17 and list those heart attitudes and behaviors that enrich your life as a Christian. What one or two areas would you like to cultivate?

Has this been a difficult lesson for you, dear one? It's always hard to face our sinful failures. But take heart as you consider some of the marvelous benefits of your obedience.

Obedience keeps our relationship with God open and free.
Obedience to God is in our best interest.
Obedience to God often keeps us from harm.
Obedience to God is pleasing to Him.
Obedience to God often leads to peace.[8]

Verses to memorize–1 Samuel 15:22 and John 14:15. Add to this list any verses that encourage you to walk in greater obedience.

Optional exercise–If you have *A Woman After God's Own Heart™ Prayer Journal*, just for today fill in the section titled "My Relationship with God" by writing out this statement and finishing it with words out of your own heart:

Lord, just for today, help me to choose Your path of obedience by...

On the following page, relate in 100 words or less one instance when you were aware that you actively chose to walk in obedience this week. Then thank God for that opportunity and His grace to make that choice.

Words from My Heart

Heart Exercise 5

A Heart That Serves

In your personal copy of *A Woman After God's Own Heart*™ read chapter 5, "A Heart That Serves." Make notes here about what meant the most to you from this chapter or offered you the greatest challenge or inspired you deeply.

♡ When I teach through the marriage chapters of *A Woman After God's Own Heart*™, I always tell the women in the classroom that there are four words in the Bible that define the role of a wife. Married or single, it benefits us to know these four words–first, for personal application, and second, to pass on to others who may need this information. The first word is found in Genesis 2:18: A wife is to *help* her husband. Read Genesis 2:18-25 and then read this explanation of Genesis 2:18:

> The words of this verse emphasize man's need for a companion, a helper, and an equal. He was incomplete without someone to complement him in fulfilling the task of filling, multiplying, and taking dominion over the earth. This points to Adam's inadequacy, not Eve's insufficiency. Woman was made by God to meet man's deficiency.[9]

Now review these words from page 59 of your book:

A helper is one who shares man's responsibilities, responds to his nature with understanding and love, and wholeheartedly cooperates with him in working out the plan of God.[10]

With these Bible definitions in mind, jot down some of the ways the world's view of a woman's role in marriage differs from God's view.

♥ As you can tell from the title above, this chapter is about serving one another, and more specifically, about serving our husbands. And, even if you're not married, a heart that serves is a reflection of Christlikeness—a quality you should desire. Write out Matthew 20:28.

What is the one word that best describes the heart of this verse?

And how does Jesus say this can be accomplished in verses 26 and 27?

♥ Now that you know you're *on assignment from God to help your husband*, and now that you have an understanding of what it means to serve others, let's look at the three suggestions made for helping your husband on pages 60-63,

1. *Make a commitment to help your husband*–I shared about the commitment I made to become a better helper to my husband. Now why don't you write out such a commitment? Be sure and keep it in your prayer journal or notebook and look at it often!

2. *Focus on your husband*–Is yours a heart that generally focuses your energy and efforts on your husband–on *his* tasks, *his* goals, *his* responsibilities–or is yours a heart that cries out, "*Me* first!"? Also, what do you plan to do, what specific actions do you plan to take, to focus on your dear husband? (You may want to draw from some of the ideas from this chapter in your book.) After you give your honest answer, read these words from another woman just like you:

> The other evening I was extremely tired and decided to relax and get a good night's rest. Well, my husband had different plans for me. After the children were put to bed, he told me he had a lot of typing to be done before the next morning. We both knew how much I dislike our particular typewriter and how tired I was (...and I did complain to myself!). But then I remembered that *I am on assignment from God to help my husband,* and began to work, which did not take as long as either one of us expected.

How about, just for today, putting these two questions to work for you with your husband?

–What can I do for you today?

–What can I do to help you make better use of your time today?

3. *Ask of your actions, "Will this help or hinder my husband?"*–Quickly look at these women in the Bible:

–*Eve* (Genesis 3:1-6,17)–Did Eve help or hinder her husband? Why...and how?

–*Sarah* (Genesis 16:1-4)–Did Sarah help or hinder her husband? Why...and how?

Can you pinpoint any situation in your marriage where your actions or attitudes may be hindering your husband? In light of the fact that you are *on assignment from God to help your husband*, what do you plan to do about this action or attitude?

Now treat yourself to a look at Priscilla, a woman who was a partner and a complement to her husband (Acts 18:24-26). How did Priscilla help her husband?

♡ As you think of your service to your husband, why not use these questions as a checklist?

✓ Do you see yourself as a team player, free of any competitive actions, thoughts, or desires?

✓ Is your husband your primary career?

✓ Is helping your husband your heart's primary concern and the main focus of your energy?

✓ Have you committed your life and your heart to following God's plan for you, His plan that you help and not hinder your husband?

One more question for those who are not married: Christlike service involves all women. How can you nurture a heart that serves those in your family, home, school, dorm, workplace, neighborhood, and church?

Verses to memorize—Matthew 20:28 and Philippians 2:3-4. Add to this list any verses that encourage you to a heart of service.

Optional exercise—If you have *A Woman After God's Own Heart™ Prayer Journal*, just for today fill in the section titled "My Husband" by writing out this statement and finishing it with words out of your own heart:

Lord, just for today, enable me to be a helper to my husband by…

On the following page, relate in 100 words or less one instance when you were aware that you actively chose to help your husband this week. Then thank God for that opportunity and His grace to make that choice.

Words from My Heart

Heart Exercise 6

A Heart That Submits

 In your personal copy of *A Woman After God's Own Heart*™ read chapter 6, "A Heart That Submits." Make notes here about what meant the most to you from this chapter or offered you the greatest challenge or inspired you deeply.

As I mentioned in the previous lesson, there are four words in the Bible that define the role of a wife. (And just so you know, we'll look at the first three words in this exercise, and the fourth word in the next.) The first word is–

#1. She is to *help* her husband.

Now let's look at God's second word to a wife–

#2. She is to *submit* to her husband.

(Or, in other words, she is *on assignment from God to submit to her husband*.) Write out what these verses say about our submission:

Ephesians 5:22-24–

Colossians 3:18–

Titus 2:5–

1 Peter 3:1 (Be sure to read verses 1-6!)–

Hopefully by now you've gained greater understanding into...

the *fact* of submission–"wives, submit to your own husbands"

the *who* of submission–"to your own husbands"

the *how* of submission–"as to the Lord"

the *when* of submission–"in everything"

the *why* of submission–"that the word of God may not be blasphemed"

And just a note: The exception to these instructions is if you are being asked to violate some teaching from God's Word (Acts 5:29). In such a situation, seek your pastor's counsel or that of another biblical counselor.

♡ *Choose a positive word of response*–Are you ready for some application? I suggested that you choose a positive word for responding to your husband. Write out the word you chose here and relate an instance when you used it. What happened?

Now read this portion of a letter I received from another wife! She writes...

> ...no sooner was our new baby boy (our ninth child!) born when my husband asked, "What about naming him Mark?" All I could utter was a single, positive word, as you recommend in *A Woman After God's Own Heart*™. I said, "Fine!" Mark really isn't one of my top favorite names but he sure is a top favorite baby!

Ask of each word, act, and attitude, "Am I bending or bucking?"—I chose this question for myself when I learned that the word *submissive* is used to describe a horse that's been tamed. My mind went wild with the image of an unsubmissive, unyielding, bucking horse (or wife, in my case!). Pinpoint a time when you chose to bend and not buck. What happened? And then read a few words from my heart to yours.

I can't tell you how many women have written—and called—to express their thoughts and feelings about my "lamp story" on page 70. I only regret, first of all, that you don't know my wonderful, godly husband, Jim. And second, that I didn't know "the end of the story" until some months after my writing of the book was finished. Here's what happened next: One day I smelled something burning, followed my nose, and found smoke rising out of that new lamp, caused by an electrical shortage in its wiring. Racing to unplug it from the wall, I noticed that the glass panels were completely blackened from the smoke and the current. The end of the story? We took the lamp back, got a full refund, and purchased another lamp with the rich colors I had wanted in the first place! Jim was honored, I grew in grace, and God, as I like to say, "burned up that lamp and supplied another one"! I hope and pray that you have many such wonderful stories to tell of your submission, your husband's exaltation, and God's grace.

Are you ready for God's third word for a wife?

#3. She is to *respect* her husband.

(Or, in other words, she's *on assignment from God to respect her husband*.)

In my early days of learning what submission to my husband meant and entailed, the following exercise was invaluable–a true eye-opener! So now I'm asking you to do the same exercise:

Using your dictionary, look up the following verbs (and one adverb) from The Amplified Bible's version of Ephesians 5:33: "And let the wife see that she *respects* her husband–that she *notices* him, *regards* him, *honors* him, *prefers* him, *venerates* and *esteems* him, and that she *defers* to him, and *praises* him, and *loves* and *admires* him *exceedingly*." Write out simple definitions here:

–respect

–notice

–regard

–honor

–prefer

–venerate

–esteem

–defer

–praise

–love

–admire

–exceedingly

Now for three "words" of application:

1. *Make a commitment to reverence and respect your husband*–
Drawing from the words and definitions above, write out a brief (no more than 10 words) motto or saying that will express an attitude of respect for your husband (for instance, "Jim's number one!" or "Jim's the greatest!"). Then make a commitment to live out your motto in daily praise and admiration.

2. *Treat your husband as you would Christ Himself.* How will you do this today?

3. *Ask of your attitude, "Am I demonstrating respect for my husband?"* Look again at Ephesians 5:33. Your respect for your husband should be obvious and active and noticeable to him and to others. How will you show your respect for him today?

Verses to memorize—Colossians 3:18 and Colossians 3:23. Add to this list any verses that encourage you to a heart of submission.

 Optional exercise—If you have *A Woman After God's Own Heart*™ *Prayer Journal*, just for today fill in the section titled "My Husband" by writing out this statement and finishing it with words out of your own heart:

Lord, just for today, help me to respond positively to my husband by...

On the following page, relate in 100 words or less one instance when you were aware that you actively chose to submit to your husband this week. Then thank God for that opportunity and His grace to make that choice.

Heart Exercise 7

A Heart That Loves, Part 1

In your personal copy of *A Woman After God's Own Heart*™ read chapter 7, "A Heart That Loves, Part 1." Make notes here about what meant the most to you from this chapter or offered you the greatest challenge or inspired you deeply.

 What does God say about the role of a wife?

> #1. She is to *help* her husband.

> #2. She is to *submit* to her husband.

> #3. She is to *respect* her husband.

As you look back over the past few weeks, how is what you're learning about helping, submitting, and respecting your husband affecting your marriage?

 Now let's look at God's fourth word to us as a wife:

> #4. She is to *love* her husband.

Read Titus 2:3-5. What message does God have for wives here?

As I explained on page 78, the love spoken of in Titus 2:4 is a love that cherishes, enjoys, and likes our husband—a friendship love. I also shared that friendship love with your husband begins as you make these two choices:

> *Decide to make your husband your number one human relationship.*

> *Begin to choose your husband over all other human relationships.*

Look again at the treatment of these two choices in your book (see pages 78-80) and evaluate your marriage to see if your priorities and choices are "out of whack." What did you determine? After you've written down your answer, see what this busy wife and mother discovered!

We have two small children, a three-year-old and a seven-month-old. It is so easy because of the amount of time spent with them to unknowingly let the other areas of your life and marriage slide. I realized that I needed to regain my focus and make my husband my VIP and give him priority over our children.

Now, let's begin to go through the nine tried-and-true ways you can express your love and build a friendship with your husband.

1. *Pray for your husband–Is your husband a Christian?* If so, begin to incorporate these scriptures into your prayers for him. Look at these verses in your Bible and make notes about what they teach.

–In the area of character qualities, look at
1 Timothy 3:1-10,12-13–

Titus 1:6-9–

–In the area of spiritual growth, look at Colossians 1:9-12–

–In the area of God's role in your husband's life, look at Philippians 1:6–

If your husband is not a Christian, pray using these scriptures often:
–In the area of God's role in your husband's life, look at
1 Timothy 2:4–

2 Peter 3:9–

–In the area of your role in your husband's life, look at
1 Corinthians 7:13–

1 Peter 3:1-6–

For all wives, in the area of your role in your husband's life, look again at these scriptures–God's four words for wives–and pray!
Help him–Genesis 2:18–

Submit to him–Ephesians 5:22-24–

Respect him–Ephesians 5:33–

Love him–Titus 2:4–

Minister to his physical needs–
1 Corinthians 7:2-5—

Proverbs 5:15-20–

Put an asterisk beside or circle any of these areas that were
new or missing from your practice and prayers for your
husband. And, because we're discussing prayer, stop and
"discuss" these matters with the Lord.

2. *Plan for your husband*–Since you are *on assignment from
God to love your husband*, try these exercises and see what
happens to your heart...and his!
–Plan a special deed of kindness for your husband each
day for a week.

–Plan a special dinner for your husband this next week.

–Plan a special date alone with your husband this week.
(If it doesn't work out with his schedule, that's OK. That
will be another opportunity for you to pay attention to
his desires and honor him. At least your heart was willing
and in the right place–and that's what this study is all
about!)

As we end this lesson, I can't help but encourage you by giving
you one more example from another woman (and wife) after
God's own heart:

> My mother had just offered us a lovely
> expense-paid weekend away as an anniversary
> present. When I happily presented this idea to
> my husband, he became very quiet. Later as
> we talked about the situation, I found that my
> husband really did not want to go away and

showed me, practically, where it was not feasible for us.

With MUCH PRAYER, I explained to my mother our appreciation of her love for us but that my husband and I were not able to accept this lovely offer. The Lord gave me the boldness to make a suggestion on what she might be able to give us, and she gratefully appreciated our truthfulness. The depth of love and communication between the family was tested, and with God's strength to obey, I believe that He was glorified through this situation.

Verses to memorize–James 5:16b and 1 John 3:18. Add to this list any verses that encourage you to pray for your husband and to love him.

Optional exercise–If you have *A Woman After God's Own Heart*™ *Prayer Journal*, just for today fill in the section titled "My Husband" by writing out this statement and finishing it with words out of your own heart:

Lord, just for today, help me to show my love to my husband by...

On the following page, relate in 100 words or less one instance when you were aware that you actively chose your husband as a priority over all others this week. Then thank God for that opportunity and His grace to make that choice.

Heart Exercise 8

A Heart That Loves, Part 2

 In your personal copy of *A Woman After God's Own Heart*™ read chapter 8, "A Heart That Loves, Part 2." Make notes here about what meant the most to you from this chapter or offered you the greatest challenge or inspired you deeply.

I hope you enjoyed looking at the first two suggestions for loving your husband that we discussed in the previous lesson–1. *Pray for him* and 2. *Plan for him*. But, there are seven more!

3. *Prepare for him daily*–If your husband were to write an article about his homecoming, what do you think he might report? Would there be any similarities with "The Homecoming" on pages 88-89?

Why not use these preparations from pages 85-89 as a checklist for measuring your husband's homecoming? Also look at any accompanying scriptures.

◇ Prepare the house–Proverbs 31:27

◇ Prepare your appearance–Proverbs 27:9a

◇ Prepare your greeting–Proverbs 12:25 and 15:30

◇ Set the table–Proverbs 9:2

◇ "The king is in the castle!"–Proverbs 31:23

◇ "The party!"

◇ Clear out all visitors

◇ Stay off the phone

◇ Prepare all the way home–Luke 6:35

◇ Pray all the way home–Ephesians 6:18 and
  1 Thessalonians 5:17

Which of these preparations for homecoming do you need to work on?

4. *Please him*–Make a list of your husband's likes and dislikes. How can you set about to please him and honor his preferences?

5. *Protect your time with him*–Does your calendar reflect more time apart than together? What changes can you make in your personal schedule to enjoy more time together?

6. *Physically love him*–Do read 1 Corinthians 7:3-5 and Proverbs 5:18-19.

7. *Positively respond to him*–Again, what positive word of response have you chosen, and are you using it? I love this "Sure!" from one of my student's homework papers.

> I don't have an example of choosing my husband over something else this week, but I was

able to give the positive response of "Sure, honey," when he asked for a second bowl of ice cream that his waistline did not need.

8. *Praise him*–Write down seven of your husband's qualities or personality traits that you admire and appreciate. Now, for the next week, praise him for one each day!

-
-
-
-

-
-
-

9. *Pray always*–Don't forget to lift prayers to God throughout your day for your husband and for your relationship with him as you seek to live out God's four words for wives.

You've done a good job working through these four chapters. I know, because of the mail I receive, just how hard they are for some of us! So I want to treat you to a couple of "stories from the heart" shared with me by women just like you who are seeking to be women after God's own heart in their marriages. Sit back, relax, and enjoy! And again, I say, "Good job!"

Eight A.M. Saturday morning! Thank goodness I have Saturdays to catch up on everything that didn't get done during the week and to leave a meal for the family while I'm at work tonight.

"Good morning, sweetheart! Sleep well? (Now what was it we were told in that pink book to ask?) What can I do to help you best use your time today?"

"What? You need to go to the nursery in Gardena and you want the kids and me to go?!!" (Quick, Shelly, think of something. You have so much to get organized before you go to work. But wait a minute. Didn't I decide to change my priorities? Remember? Dave [husband] first. Housework can wait. So what if you'll be gone until it's time to go to work? Quick, say something positive!)

"Okay honey, sure, we'd all love to go!!" (What have I just done?!)

P.S. The housework didn't get done. Ronald McDonald fed my family that night, but choosing to do what Dave asked was a victory for me. (I didn't say anything negative!) We were blessed with a happy time together that day!

~~~~~~~~~~~

One day two women approached me at a book-signing and asked me to autograph their battered copies of *A Woman After God's Own Heart*™. As I was writing out an inscription to each of them, I learned that they were mother and daughter. The daughter elbowed her mother and said, "Mom, why don't you tell Elizabeth about what Dad said last week?"

Well, now it was Mom's turn. She related how her husband had gone for a physical exam in preparation for his retirement. Several weeks later, he sat her down and announced, "Honey, I have to ask you something important. Am I dying?"

"Why, honey, why would you ask that?!"

"Well," came his answer, "you know I went for my physical and I haven't heard back from the doctor. I just thought maybe he had called you with bad news and you didn't tell me. You've been so nice to me recently that I thought I must be dying."

This story is funny…and yet again it isn't! Do you see, dear one, what our obedience to God's four words to us as wives—help, submit, respect, and love—can mean to our beloved husbands? I thank God for a wife who, even in her retirement years, would make such dramatic and noticeable changes, who would make God's standards her own. I can only imagine the joy her husband must have experienced in his heart as he learned that not only was he *not* dying, but that he had a transformed wife and marriage! What a gift we give to our husbands when we communicate "I love you" God's way. As we finish these lessons on being a wife after God's own heart, let's get to work showing our husbands the love that's in our hearts!

 Verses to memorize—Proverbs 12:4 and 1 John 3:18. Add to this list any verses that encourage you to pray for your husband and to love him.

 Optional exercise—If you have *A Woman After God's Own Heart*™ *Prayer Journal*, just for today fill in the section titled "My Husband" by writing out this statement and finishing it with words out of your own heart:

Lord, just for today, help me to show my love to my husband by…

On the following page, relate in 100 words or less one instance when you were aware that you actively chose to show love to your husband this week. Then thank God for that opportunity and His grace to make that choice.

Heart Exercise 9

A Heart That Values Being a Mother

 In your personal copy of *A Woman After God's Own Heart*™ read chapter 9, "A Heart That Values Being a Mother." Make notes here about what meant the most to you from this chapter or offered you the greatest challenge or inspired you deeply.

♥ As we launch into this section on mothering, I hope you'll notice that we are moving–in order–through the priorities that God sets down for us in His Word. Of course, God is Number One, "for in Him we live and move and have our being" (Acts 17:28). Look again at Titus 2:3-5. What is the first "topic" (or priority) on the curriculum list that the older women are to teach the younger women (verse 4)?

And what is the second topic (verse 4)?

Now that we've spent time considering our love for God and for our husbands, let's see what God's Word says about our children and the passions that reflect a heart that values being a mother.

♡   *A passion for teaching God's Word*–First make notes
regarding the teaching of Proverbs 1:8 and Proverbs 6:20.
Next, look at a mother and grandmother–Eunice and
Lois–who took their assignment from God to teach His
Word to their young Timothy seriously. As you may know,
Timothy was a co-worker and personal representative of
the apostle Paul to the Ephesian church. And note, too,
that Timothy's father and Eunice's husband was probably
an unbeliever (Acts 16:1).

2 Timothy 1:5–Describe Timothy's faith and its source.

2 Timothy 3:15–What is one role Eunice and Lois
played in Timothy's early childhood, and what did their
teaching help accomplish?

As you consider these two women after God's own heart
and the impact that their faithful teaching of God's Word
had upon a young child, what steps (or additional steps)
are you going to take to ensure that your children, too,
know the Scriptures from childhood? (Remember, as a
mother you are *on assignment from God to teach His Word to
your children!*)

♡   *A passion for teaching God's wisdom*–Not only are we to
teach the actual Word of God to our children, but we are
also to teach them practical, scriptural wisdom for daily
life. To witness a mother involved in such teaching, look
at Proverbs 31:1-9. Who is the mother?

And who is the "pupil"?

Make a brief list of the practical areas of life covered by this faithful, passionate mother in verses 3-9.

And what practical area of life is included in verses 10-31?

♡ *The place for teaching God's Word and wisdom*—We tend to think first of taking our children to church to be taught God's Word and wisdom (and there is certainly a place for that, as we'll soon see), but consider the "classroom scene" God describes in Deuteronomy 6:6-7:

Before any teaching can take place, where must the Word of God first reside?

What urgent command is given by God to parents?

What four scenes of daily life does God paint as the setting for teaching our children?

What can you do to turn the daily activities of life into a classroom for teaching God's Word and wisdom? Think of as many as you can. Use the back pages in this book or an extra page of paper if you must. Then check off two or three that you can begin *today!* Oh, please don't wait another day or minute to begin this vital ministry to your dear children!

♡   Now for some practical "how-to's."

Make some serious decisions—Or, put another way, "Will you or won't you make a commitment to choose to teach God's Word and wisdom to your children?" Why not write such a commitment here or in your prayer journal?

Recognize your role of teacher—Yes, this role will be costly and sacrifices will have to be made, but, as an Italian proverb says, "A teacher is like the candle, which lights others in consuming itself." Do you see yourself as a teacher of God's truth to your children? Or does the thought of "teaching" them about God make you feel awkward, nervous, incompetent? Or are you afraid your family will think you are "stupid," that studying the Bible is a "dumb" idea? Or do you think your little one is too little? Answer honestly about what keeps you from this duty. Each day in your prayer time, own this awesome role, ask God for His help to faithfully live it out, and just do it! Do it badly! Do it "dumbly." Do it when your kids don't care or want you to do it. But, whatever you do and however you do it, *do it!!!!!*

Consider these examples–How did the stories of Jochebed, Hannah, and Mary encourage you in your role as a teacher of truth to your children?

Memorize scripture and read the Bible together–What are you doing or could you do in this vital area of spiritual training?

Follow the model of other mothers–Pick out several women in your church who are making strides in this area of biblical and spiritual mothering. What can you do to duplicate their efforts?

How about one more exercise? Design a daily schedule that includes a time in God's Word with your children. Then set out what you'll need (a Bible, a teen devotional book, workbook or activity book, a little book of prayers, books about Jesus, books about Bible characters, songbooks or sing-along tapes, memory cards, etc.). Utter a prayer, and then make sure you and your precious ones keep that appointment. Write out your initial plan here.

When will we meet?

Where will we meet?

What will we do?

And for how long?

 Verses to memorize—Deuteronomy 6:6-7. Add to this list any verses that encourage you in your role of teaching God's Word and wisdom to your children and grandchildren.

 Optional exercise—If you have *A Woman After God's Own Heart™ Prayer Journal*, just for today fill in the section titled "My Children" by writing out this statement and finishing it with words out of your own heart:

Lord, just for today, help me to be faithful to impart Your Word and Your wisdom to my children by…

On the following page, relate in 100 words or less one instance when you actively chose having a time with your children in God's Word as a priority over other activities. Then thank God for His grace to make that choice.

Words from My Heart

THE PURSUIT OF GOD'S PRIORITIES—HER CHILDREN

Heart Exercise 10

A Heart That Prays Faithfully

In your personal copy of *A Woman After God's Own Heart*™ read chapter 10, "A Heart That Prays Faithfully." Make notes here about what meant the most to you from this chapter or offered you the greatest challenge or inspired you deeply.

I hope your heart was stirred to action as you completed our previous study about appreciating the value of being a mother. And I hope your passions—more specifically, *a passion for teaching God's Word* and *a passion for teaching God's wisdom*—grew to embrace God's assignment to teach His Word to your children. This exercise will hopefully light a fresh fire under two more passions. First...

♥ *A passion for prayer*—Look at Proverbs 31:2 and write out your Bible's translation of this verse.

Now read in 1 Samuel 1:1-10 about the life of Hannah, a woman who prayed faithfully. Make a note of Hannah's problems.

What did her difficulties lead her to do in verse 10?

Now read verses 11-20. In addition to pouring out her heart in prayer, what additional action did she take in verse 11?

Hannah was faithful to pray (and to vow!), and God blessed her and gave her a son, little Samuel. Read about another step of faithfulness in the life of Hannah in verses 21-28. What was that step?

Next read 1 Samuel 2:1-11. According to verse 1, what did Hannah do when she delivered her small son to Eli, the priest, at the temple of the Lord, and what were her opening words (verse 2)?

Hannah's example teaches that in every event or difficulty we are to pray, focusing our heart and mind on the person and power of God, not on our circumstances. Just like Hannah, you can be confident of God's sovereign and loving control over the events of your life–and the lives of your children! As Hannah's lips reveal her heart in verses 1-10, note the content of Hannah's impassioned prayer:

–God's salvation–

–God's holiness–

–God's strength–

–God's knowledge–

–God's power–

–God's judgment–

How do these scenes from the life of this mother who prayed faithfully instruct and challenge you about your prayer life and speak to you as a mother?

♡ *A passion for godly training*–It's one thing to talk to your children about the Lord and to talk to the Lord about your children, but there are other steps we can and must take in the area of godly training. These steps are costly and involve personal sacrifice on your part, but God's kind of training takes time and dedication. What level of commitment are you making and willing to make in these areas of godly training?

–Church attendance–

–Sunday school attendance–

–Church outings and camps–

–Youth groups and Bible studies–

Exposure to God's truth and the opportunity to be with other strong believers awaits your children when you make the effort to take these steps. I have in my teaching notes a clever article titled "Generations of Excuses."[11] Take a look at this series of excuses for not getting little ones to church that spanned two generations.

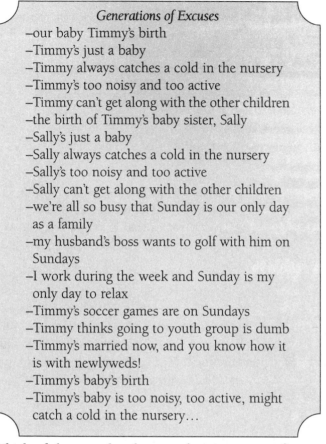

Generations of Excuses

–our baby Timmy's birth
–Timmy's just a baby
–Timmy always catches a cold in the nursery
–Timmy's too noisy and too active
–Timmy can't get along with the other children
–the birth of Timmy's baby sister, Sally
–Sally's just a baby
–Sally always catches a cold in the nursery
–Sally's too noisy and too active
–Sally can't get along with the other children
–we're all so busy that Sunday is our only day as a family
–my husband's boss wants to golf with him on Sundays
–I work during the week and Sunday is my only day to relax
–Timmy's soccer games are on Sundays
–Timmy thinks going to youth group is dumb
–Timmy's married now, and you know how it is with newlyweds!
–Timmy's baby's birth
–Timmy's baby is too noisy, too active, might catch a cold in the nursery...

Which of these tend to be your favorite excuses for not getting your family to church?

It's God's job to work in our children's hearts and lives, but it's our job to expose them to others who will teach them the truth. Are you committed to getting your children to church so they can be exposed to the truth, no matter what it costs? What would it cost you this week?

In Heart Exercise #2, we talked about the value of saying "no" to things that are pleasant, profitable, and good if they would hinder or clog our grand duties and our chief work. What can you say "no" to this week in order to

—spend more time in prayer for your children?

—see that your children get to church?

 Verses to memorize—James 5:16b (again!), Hebrews 10:25, and Proverbs 22:6. Add to this list any verses that encourage you in your role of training your children and grandchildren.

Optional exercise—If you have *A Woman After God's Own Heart™ Prayer Journal*, just for today fill in the section titled "My Children" by writing out this statement and finishing it with words out of your own heart:

Lord, just for today, help me to spend extra time praying for my children's...

On the following page, relate in 100 words or less one instance when you actively chose praying for your children as a priority over other activities. Then thank God for His grace to make that choice.

Words from My Heart

The Pursuit of God's Priorities—
Her Children

Heart Exercise 11

A Heart Overflowing with
Motherly Affection, Part 1

 In your personal copy of *A Woman After God's Own Heart*™ read chapter 11, "A Heart Overflowing with Motherly Affection, Part 1." Make notes here about what meant the most to you from this chapter or offered you the greatest challenge or inspired you deeply.

♡ We've dealt with some pretty serious topics in this section on mothering, haven't we? It was sobering to consider our need to develop a passion for teaching God's Word, for wisdom, for prayer, and for godly training. But mothering is made up of other things as well. Look at Titus 2:4 again. Just as we're on assignment to love our husbands with a friendship love–to like them, to be their friend–so we're to love our children in the same way. So, let's look at ten marks of motherly affection–ten ways to live out our assignment from God to love them. We'll examine five in this exercise and five in the next.

1. *A heart that prays*–Did you enjoy the poem about a praying mother? I know it's one of my favorites. In fact, I can just about recite it from memory. Well, here's another one that is quite touching.

> *Baby Shoes*
> Often tiny baby feet, tired from their play,
> Kick off scuffed-up little shoes
>   at the close of day.
> And often tired mothers find them lying there,
> And over them send up to God
>   this fervent, whispered prayer:
>
> "God, guide his every footstep
>   in paths where Thou has stood;
> God, make him brave; God, make him strong;
> And please, God, make him good!"[12]

Now, what kind of prayers are you praying for your dear children? Jot down a few notes of their general contents here.

2. *A heart that provides*–Read Proverbs 31:10-31, listing the provisions this godly mother made for her family.

Are there any "basics" your children are missing out on at home? What will you do this week to remedy this situation so that yours is a heart overflowing with motherly affection?

3. *A heart that is happy*–I know that we've already looked at this scripture in our study, but please write out again the

teaching of Proverbs 12:25. How can your happy heart and a good word minister to your family? And, the opposite, how can your lack of a happy heart and a good word affect them negatively?

Now look at a few more proverbs:

Proverbs 15:13–

Proverbs 15:15–

Proverbs 17:22–

Does being cheerful and being "up" and "lighting up" for your family sound unimportant? Hypocritical? Impossible? Read on...

> When you mentioned in class this semester that we should be "up" for our family, I struggled. I wondered, "Can we really do that and be real?" And as I began to try and make the effort for my family, I discovered that, with my eyes off myself and onto God, I could. This opened me up to viewing my family differently and allowed God to show me the dream of making our home delightful. This perspective has changed *my* attitude in the day-to-day things I am doing for my family, and it has begun transforming *me!*

Why not plan to be "up" for your family today? Why not "light up" when you see them? Why not plan the "good word" you will give right now? I remember hearing writer and teacher Elisabeth Elliot share on a tape that as the homemaker, "*you* create the atmosphere of the home with *your* attitudes." And your happiness is a powerful influence!

4. *A heart that gives*–Closely related to a heart that is happy is a heart that gives. Look at these verses in your Bible and write out in a few words how each encourages you to nurture a heart that gives.

John 3:16–

Mark 10:45–

On page 121, I made a list of some ways that you and I can be "the giver." We can give…

–the smile
–the cheerful greeting
–the hug
–the compliment
–the encouragement
–the praise
–the time
–the listening ear
–the ride
–the extra mile

Jot down beside each one of these evidences of motherly affection some specific effort you can make to give these priceless gifts to your children this week.

5. *A heart of fun*–Just for fun, consider doing one of the following this week.

–check out a riddle book from the library
–read the newspaper cartoons together with your children

–have a "tickle time"

–have a pillow fight

–go out for a "fun" time that's not connected with any errands

–ask other mothers for their "fun" ideas

Think of three or four ideas yourself and add them to this list

   –

   –

   –

   –

Verses to memorize–Mark 10:45 and Proverbs 12:25. Add to this list any verses that encourage you in your role of affectionately loving your children and grandchildren.

Optional exercise–If you have *A Woman After God's Own Heart™ Prayer Journal*, just for today fill in the section titled "My Children" by writing out this statement and finishing it with words out of your own heart:

Lord, just for today, help my heart to overflow with motherly affection by...

On the following page, relate in 100 words or less one instance when you actively chose to give motherly affection to your children. Then thank God for His grace to make that choice.

Heart Exercise 12

A Heart Overflowing with Motherly Affection, Part 2

 In your personal copy of *A Woman After God's Own Heart*™ read chapter 12, "A Heart Overflowing with Motherly Affection, Part 2." Make notes here about what meant the most to you from this chapter or offered you the greatest challenge or inspired you deeply.

🤍 I hope you enjoyed the first five "heart exercises" that should propel you and me further down the road to being a mom whose heart overflows with motherly affection. Are you ready for five more?

6. *A heart that celebrates*–Write out Matthew 5:41 here.

When you think of the "first mile" of your job assignment from God as a mother, what comes to mind? (Don't forget to incorporate what you've been learning in the three previous chapters.)

Turning the mundane into a celebration–this is one way we as mothers can go *the extra mile*. Can you think of the many mundane activities your family will face today or in the next week? Note several here, and write out a plan for making these routine events a celebration.

7. *A heart that gives preferential treatment*–Look again at Titus 2:3-5. How important do you think your children are as you consider God's words to women in this passage?

A good way to express to your children that they take priority in your heart is to practice the principle, *Don't give away to others what you have not first given away at home.* List three ways you can communicate to your children the high priority they have in your heart. What can you do to show your children that they are more important to you than other people?

8. *A heart that is focused*–Look next at Matthew 6:24 and write it out here.

Now consider my principle, *Beware of double-booking*. Looking at this past week, can you pinpoint any instances where you may have tried to double-book? What happened? What did you hope to accomplish when you double-booked? How did it turn out? After you've written about your experience, read what another mother just like you wrote.

Well, it finally happened! God is dealing with my telephone habits! This week we talked about not neglecting our children by double-booking. With two little ones, the phone has been my line to the adult world. But when I realized the importance of my role as their mother and started to think of all the possibilities of things I could do with them to teach them, play with them, and "have a ball" as a family, the phone lost its influence in my life.

Its jingling interruptions are now handled by "Igor," our prerecorded message answering machine. With Igor on duty 'round the clock now, I can answer and return calls at nap time. I know that I'm doing the right thing.

9. *A heart that is present*—After reading this section of your book, were there any new issues to think about? What were they?

What are some of the activities that tend to take you away from your family and home at night?

Evaluate these activities, spend time in prayer with God about them this next week, talk these things over with your husband, and begin to make the choices that bless your family. Then…watch for the blessings!

Speaking of blessings, consider this next quality!

10. *A heart that is quiet*—Write out Proverbs 31:26.

What are the two "laws" that govern this godly wife and mother's speech?

When you speak to your children or to others about them, do your words tend to match up to the biblical standard set here in Proverbs 31:26 or do you need to make some changes? Please explain.

What is the instruction to us as women in 1 Timothy 3:11?

And Titus 2:3?

And, another of my favorites, Titus 3:2.

Now, how do these exhortations regarding gossip and slander relate to us as mothers?

I hope you are at least *thinking* about ways to express your love to your dear children! None of these exercises is overwhelming, and each is lived out in the daily minutia of life. But, dear woman after God's own heart, packaged together, the many little things we do send a loud and clear message of love to every precious person under your roof, such as this woman relates.

I know I put my children as a priority last Thursday. I began my day by asking the Lord to help me make it special for my kids and my husband. I prayed for them as often as I could throughout the day. I went grocery shopping and made a special meal and dessert for that night. We had special dishes and a candle for the setting. (Ironically, it was my husband who thought that was neat!) The Lord gave me special time and special thoughts for each of them. It truly was a blessed day in every way. Joy abounded!

 Verses to memorize—Matthew 6:24 and Proverbs 31:26. Add to this list any verses that encourage you in your role of affectionately loving your children and grandchildren.

 Optional exercise—If you have *A Woman After God's Own Heart™ Prayer Journal*, just for today fill in the section titled "My Children" by writing out this statement and finishing it with words out of your own heart:

Lord, just for today, help my heart to overflow with motherly affection by...

On the following page, relate in 100 words or less one instance when you actively chose to give motherly affection to your children. Then thank God for His grace to make that choice.

Words from My Heart

Heart Exercise 13

A Heart That Makes a House a Home

 In your personal copy of *A Woman After God's Own Heart*™ read Chapter 13, "A Heart That Makes a House a Home." Make notes here about what meant the most to you from this chapter or offered you the greatest challenge or inspired you deeply.

♡ *The business of building*–To gain a better understanding of what it means to make a house a home, write out Proverbs 14:1.

–Creating the atmosphere. As we start, take the temperature of your own home. Share a few words that describe typical daily life under your roof.

Now look up these scriptures and check the ones that you most need to apply in order to build your home into all that you and God want it to be.

◇ Proverbs 12:25–

◇ Proverbs 15:1–

◇ Proverbs 15:13–

◇ Proverbs 15:15–

◇ Proverbs 15:18–

◇ Proverbs 16:24–

◇ Proverbs 31:26–

—Building a refuge. Just this morning an email sister sent me this quote, which she called "another spiritual nugget":

> When the pressures of the world intrude,
> there is no shelter like a peaceful home.

What specific steps can you take to make your home a shelter, a haven, a refuge, a retreat, a hospital for your loved ones, to build your home into what God wants it to be?

–Avoiding the negatives. As we took apart Proverbs 14:1 (on pages 134-138), we noted that there are (at least!) two ways a woman can put her home-building at risk. Jot down what comes to your mind in each category.

1. Active (working destruction)–

2. Passive (failing to work)–

♡ *Carrying out the building process*–You and I both want what God wants–a home that honors Him and creates for our loved ones a little bit of heaven on earth. Here are the ways to begin the building process that brings about such a "home sweet home."

–Understand that wisdom builds. We've talked about "wisdom" throughout this book, so I thought this would be a good place to insert a working definition of wisdom.

> *Wisdom* is the ability to use the best means at the best time to accomplish the best ends. It is not merely a matter of information or knowledge, but of skillful and practical application of the truth to the ordinary facets of life.[13]

(I have to admit, "good…better…best" immediately comes to my mind!) What do you think the key words of this definition are, and why?

Which area of this definition challenges you most? Or, put another way, do you need more knowledge, more skills, or more careful diligence to application? Then share what you plan to do about any weak areas.

–Decide to begin building. We also discussed making a commitment for doing the work involved in home-building. Look at these two scriptures and write out how they apply to creating an enchanted oasis called home.

* Proverbs 31:13–

* Colossians 3:23–

"Commit your works to the LORD and your thoughts [and plans] will be established" (Proverbs 16:3). Why not write out a fresh commitment right now, committing your works, thoughts, plans, and dreams about your home to the Lord and asking for His grace to enable you in your home-building endeavors?

–Each day do one thing to build your home. On page 140, I wrote,

> Look around your home (or apartment or room or half a room), inside and out. Make a list of the things that need to be added, repaired, set up, etc. so that your home is more of a refuge. Then do one item on your list each day–or even one each week.

If you haven't already made such a list, do so now, and put it in your prayer journal or notebook or some other important place. (Remember our definition of wisdom? It's not merely a matter of information or knowledge, but of skillful and practical application of the truth to the ordinary facets of life—like homemaking!)

Verses to memorize—Proverbs 14:1 and Proverbs 31:27. Add to this list any verses that encourage you in your role of homemaker.

Optional exercise—If you have *A Woman After God's Own Heart™ Prayer Journal*, just for today fill in the section titled "My Home" by writing out this statement and finishing it with words out of your own heart:

Lord, just for today, help me to make my house a home by...

On the following page, relate in 100 words or less one instance when you actively chose to work (willingly and heartily!) on your home. Then thank God for His grace to make that choice.

(Just a reminder: How is your Quiet Times Calendar looking? Your homemaking will benefit greatly from taking care of your *spiritual* housekeeping!)

Heart Exercise 14

A Heart That Watches Over the Home

 In your personal copy of *A Woman After God's Own Heart*™ read chapter 14, "A Heart That Watches Over the Home." Make notes here about what meant the most to you from this chapter or offered you the greatest challenge or inspired you deeply.

We ended our last lesson by memorizing Proverbs 31:27. Can you write it out from memory here as we begin to unpack its riches?

Watching–How was "watching" (from Proverbs 31:27) defined and described on page 144?

Like a shepherdess, the woman with a heart that watches over her home looks well to the "ways" or "paths" or "tracks" of her home and those who live there. What does Psalm 23:3 say about God's watchcare over your "ways" or "paths" or "tracks"?

Like the Lord, our Shepherd, a homemaker after God's own heart carefully notices the patterns of her home life, the general comings and goings, the habits and activities of the people at home. The Hebrew word for "ways" means "literal tracks made by constant use." They're like the footpath that cuts across a lawn due to repeated use. Would you say that you are "watching" well over your loved ones and are aware of their "ways"? Why or why not?

Are there any "ways" developing that you are not pleased with, that don't seem to honor God's standards? What can and will you do about them?

Working—As we head into this section, I hope you know that we're not addressing working outside the home at a job. No, this has to do with the work you do *inside* the house, *at* home, the work that turns your house into a *home*. On pages 143 and 144, I mentioned that I had gone through a Bible study on the topic of "Why Work?" Why don't we do our own study on this same question and ethic right now? Of course, we'll want to look at some wonderful proverbs! Take notes on what God teaches us about work through them.

Proverbs 10:4–

Proverbs 12:11–

Proverbs 14:23–

Proverbs 18:9–

Proverbs 20:13–

Proverbs 28:19–

Proverbs 31:13–

Proverbs 31:27–

Now look at the picture God paints for us in Proverbs 24:30-34. What is His message?

Just one more verse from Ecclesiastes 9:10a–

As you "sit" and "consider" and "look at" and "receive instruction" (Proverbs 24:32) from these verses which represent only a small portion of what the Bible teaches us about the benefits and how-to's of working diligently, list two or three loud messages to your heart.

Now, make a schedule for the upcoming week that incorporates some of the Bible's wise advice regarding your work habits.

Working out your watching and working–Write out again Proverbs 14:1, and then let's look at some ways to follow through on God's design for us as home-builders who watch over the place and the people at home and do the work that brings God's plan to life.

–Step One: Understand that your role as helper and guard is God's plan for you. This is a good place to consider the word "virtuous" (Proverbs 31:10). What were the components of its definition as stated on page 146?

How does God's calling to be a "virtuous" woman help you to understand and embrace your God-given role as a helper to those *in* your home and a guard *over* your home?

–Step Two: Begin watching over your home. Do you need to spend some time in prayer about this vital step? Do you need to ask God to help you take this step?

–Step Three: Eliminate idleness. I know we've spent a lot of time on the first half of Proverbs 31:27, but write out the second part again.

Can you think of three real ways you can eliminate idleness today...and in the week (and weeks!) to come?

1.

2.

3.

As we close this lesson on the loving watchcare you and I can minister to our dear families, I just can't resist sharing this short-but-to-the-point testimony from another woman after God's own heart. She's added yet another element to this three-step formula—indeed, *the* element!

> This last week I purposed to be more "domestically inclined"! It occurred to me to PRAY about my house and housework—I never had before. But what a difference! Everything gets done more efficiently when I've brought it before the Lord and when He's helping me manage IT instead of IT managing me.

 Verses to memorize—Proverbs 14:23 and Proverbs 31:10. Add to this list any verses that encourage you in your role of homemaker.

 Optional exercise—If you have *A Woman After God's Own Heart™ Prayer Journal*, just for today fill in the section titled "My Home" by writing out this statement and finishing it with words out of your own heart:

Lord, just for today, help me to "build" my house by…

On the following page, relate in 100 words or less one instance when you actively chose to take your role as a watcher and worker seriously this week. Then thank God for His grace to make that choice.

Words from My Heart

Heart Exercise 15

A Heart That Creates Order from Chaos

In your personal copy of *A Woman After God's Own Heart*™ read chapter 15, "A Heart That Creates Order from Chaos." Make notes here about what meant the most to you from this chapter or offered you the greatest challenge or inspired you deeply.

♥ *Responsibility and accountability*–Read 1 Timothy 5:13-14. As the apostle Paul observed the behavior of the young widows of his day, what distressing habits did he list in verse 13?

What did he say was "better" for these women (verse 14)?

♥ *Understanding God's best for us*–God's desire that we build and watch over and manage a home is obviously not only "better" for us, but also "best." (We can thus be sure that those who dwell under our roof will enjoy the beauty of order versus the confusion of chaos!) What does Titus 2:3-5 have to say on this subject?

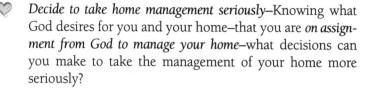

Decide to take home management seriously–Knowing what God desires for you and your home–that you are *on assignment from God to manage your home*–what decisions can you make to take the management of your home more seriously?

Twelve tips for time management–Hopefully by now you've turned the level of your commitment to your home up a notch...or two! Now, let's look at some practical tips that will help us with our good-housekeeping chores. Write out one goal for next week in each of these areas. Then, at the end of your week, see how many you can check off as accomplished.

◇ #1. Plan in detail–My goal:

◇ #2. Deal with today–My goal:

◇ #3. Value each minute–My goal:

> **Just a Minute**
> I have only just a minute—
> Just sixty seconds in it;
> Forced upon me—can't refuse it,
> didn't seek it, didn't choose it.
> But it is up to me to use it.
> I must suffer if I lose it,
> give account if I abuse it;
> Just a tiny little minute...
> but eternity is in it![14]

◇ #4. Keep moving–My goal:

◇ #5. Develop a routine–My goal:

◇ #6. Exercise and diet–My goal:

◇ #7. Ask the "half-the-time"question–My goal:

◇ #8. Use a timer for everything–My goal:

◇ #9. Do the worst first–My goal:

◇ #10.Read daily on time management–My goal:

◇ #11. Say no–My goal:

> We must say "no" not only to things which are wrong and sinful, but to things pleasant, profitable, and good which would hinder and clog our grand duties and our chief work.[15]

◇ #12. Begin the night before–My goal:

Verses to memorize–Psalm 90:12 and Luke 16:10. Add to this list any verses that encourage you in your role of homemaker.

 Optional exercise–If you have *A Woman After God's Own Heart*™ *Prayer Journal*, just for today fill in the section titled "My Home" by writing out this statement and finishing it with words out of your own heart:

Lord, just for today, help me to better manage my home by…

On the following page, relate in 100 words or less one instance when you actively chose to put your energy and efforts to work at home. Then thank God for His grace to make that choice.

Words from My Heart

Heart Exercise 16

A Heart That Weaves a Tapestry of Beauty

 In your personal copy of *A Woman After God's Own Heart*™ read chapter 16, "A Heart That Weaves a Tapestry of Beauty." Make notes here about what meant the most to you from this chapter or offered you the greatest challenge or inspired you deeply.

💜 *The priority of home*—As we've been moving through this book and our priorities, we've looked often at Titus 2:3-5. We learned that, after loving God with all our heart, soul, mind, and strength, we are to learn (and the older women are to teach others) how to love our *husbands* and love our *children*. Look once again at Titus 2:3-5. How does your version of the Bible state Paul's exhortation regarding your home? Write it out here. Then look at some other Bible translations of this same exhortation.

For the past three lessons we've focused on building our home and watching over our home and working on our home. We've concentrated on learning what this means and how to do it. And we've been challenged to do it better and do it faster. All summed up, these threads–the knowledge of God's truth, a right attitude in your heart, and the skills in motion–make up the beginnings of a beautiful tapestry, a tapestry called "home." Let's look at a few more threads now.

♥ *Understand the beauty and blessings of God's will for you*–As you take God's role of homemaker more seriously, not only will your home be more orderly and lovely, but there will be added spiritual blessings, as this woman shared in a letter.

> Recently I made a very important decision to be home more often! Let me share some of the many blessings I've already experienced. First, I've been able to begin practicing God's role for me as a woman and to CONSISTENTLY spend time in prayer. I've begun to realize how important my family and home are and what a ministry God has given me there. What a blessing it is to say to my son, "What is it I can pray about for you today?" To have him see answers to those prayers is worth any sacrifice. My husband, too, commented on how a situation at work had begun to get better because of prayer. I now realize the importance of the family and home and what God can do when we CHOOSE to allow Him to work in our home and in our lives. I now have a full-time ministry to my family.

And *you*? What blessings are you and your family beginning to reap as you understand more about God's priorities and make the choices that reflect them? As the hymn reminds us:

"Count your blessings; Name them one by one.
Count your many blessings; See what God hath done."

Understand that homemaking can be learned–I was fortunate to find sisters in Christ to help me learn a few good housekeeping tips. Do you need a little help? Some instruction from someone who's doing a good job of weaving their tapestry of beauty? Pinpoint a few areas where some assistance would be valuable.

Now, what can you do today and in the upcoming week to move toward getting the help you need?

And one more question–Do you own a good book on homemaking or know where to borrow one? Write down the titles of several helpful books here. Also ask others for their favorites.

Be home more often–This may sound repetitious, but being at home more often is at the heart of your homemaking. The old saying, "Absence makes the heart grow fonder," is *not* true when it comes to your home! Look at your calendar for last week and note these facts:

How many meetings did you have?

How many outings did you have?

How many get-togethers did you have?

How many lunches out did you have?

How many appointments did you have?

How many evenings out did you have?

How many days did you run errands?

(For some of us, we might ask, "How many hours was I home?!")

Now that the truth is in, make a schedule for the up-coming week that allows you to be home more often.

 Organize your outings—What does Ephesians 5:15-16 say about time?

How do you think organizing your outings will help you and your loved ones reap more blessings in your home?

In my book, *Beautiful in God's Eyes—The Treasures of the Proverbs 31 Woman*, I ended the chapter on Proverbs 31:27, "A Watchful Eye," with these words:

> I know it may not seem very inviting or sound very exciting, but your home is definitely the place most worthy of your diligent watching. In fact, home is the most important place in the world for you to be spending your time and investing your energy. Why do I say that? Because the work you do in "a little place" like home is eternal work, meaningful work, important work—when you realize that the work you do in your home is your supreme service to God! I invite you to enjoy the beauty of serving in a little place, a little place…like home.

A Little Place

"Where shall I work today, dear Lord?"
And my love flowed warm and free.
He answered and said,
"See that little place?
Tend that place for Me."

I answered and said, "Oh no, not there!
No one would ever see.
No matter how well my work was done,
Not that place for me!"

His voice, when He spoke, was soft and kind,
He answered me tenderly,
"Little one, search that heart of thine,
Are you working for them or ME?
Nazareth was a little place...
So was Galilee."[16]

Verses to memorize–Proverbs 17:24 and Ephesians 5:15-16. Add to this list any verses that encourage you in your role of homemaker.

Optional exercise–If you have *A Woman After God's Own Heart™ Prayer Journal*, just for today fill in the section titled "My Home" by writing out this statement and finishing it with words out of your own heart:

Lord, just for today, help me to make my home a high priority by...

On the following page, relate in 100 words or less one instance when you actively chose to be at home. Then thank God for His grace to make that choice.

Words from My Heart

Heart Exercise 17

A Heart Strengthened by Spiritual Growth

In your personal copy of *A Woman After God's Own Heart*™ read chapter 17, "A Heart Strengthened by Spiritual Growth." Make notes here about what meant the most to you from this chapter or offered you the greatest challenge or inspired you deeply.

We're nearing the end of our study of what the Bible says about priorities for us as women after God's own heart. Are you perhaps wondering, "But what about *me*? Where do *I* fit in all of this?" This whole book has been about others, and as we address the area of "self," I want you to know that whenever I speak of "self" I have one thing in mind, and one thing only–preparing your "self" so that your life overflows in ministry into the lives of others. "Self" is merely the mainspring to ministry. "Self" is growth—spiritual growth and personal growth—so that others are blessed by your efforts to grow. Let's consider some of the facets of spiritual growth.

♥ *Spiritual growth begins in Jesus Christ*–Note the "facts" about eternal life found in 1 John 5:11-12.

Now answer as honestly as you can–Do you have the Son of God? Do you have eternal life? And why do you answer in this way?

If you cannot answer "yes," ask God to begin to move you toward a complete knowledge of Him, His Son, and your sin. You might want to write out a prayer here.

Spiritual growth involves the pursuit of knowledge–Look at Proverbs 15:14 in your Bible and copy it here. Don't forget to note the contrast it gives us.

What five areas would you like to begin growing in? List them and then set up your five file folders. These will now be known as your "five fat files." Congratulations on taking a crucial growth step that few ever take!

1.

2.

3.

4.

5.

Spiritual growth includes stewardship of your body–Look at 1 Corinthians 9:27 in your Bible.

How did Paul treat and view his body?

How can a failure to discipline your body affect the quality of your life?

We mentioned both diet and exercise as areas requiring discipline. Set a goal for each for the upcoming week.

Diet–

Exercise–

 Spiritual growth means becoming like Jesus–What is Peter's exhortation in 2 Peter 3:18?

On pages 177-178 I likened spiritual growth to preparing a meal for your family. Do you have such a plan for growing in knowledge? Can you share it here? For instance...

What "thing" are you doing?

And in what place?

And with what study tools?

And at what time?

Also, how does your Quiet Times Calendar look?

♥ *Spiritual growth blesses others*–Do you agree or disagree that your mind, mouth, and manners can mar or minister to others, and why?

–Your mind. How important is your thought life according to Proverbs 23:7?

What does Philippians 4:8 suggest for your thought life?

Set a goal for your thoughts about others.

–Your mouth. Look again at Proverbs 31:26. What are two guidelines we should establish for the words we speak?

What are several other guidelines found in Ephesians 4:29?

And what ultimate guideline does the psalmist set for our mouth (and for our mind, too) in Psalm 19:14?

Set a goal for your speech to and about others.

–Your manners. Romans 12:10 gives us guidelines for the manner in which we should treat others. What are they?

Now look at Philippians 2:3-5. What is the message of verse 3?

And of verse 4?

And of verse 5?

Set a goal for your manners toward others.

–Mary and Martha. We've already discussed these two sisters, but look again at Luke 10:38-42. How did their actions, attitudes, and words reveal what was going on in their hearts?

	Mary	*Martha*
Mind		
Mouth		
Manners		

Again, what steps can you take to be more like Mary and less like Martha?

Verses to memorize–Psalm 19:14 and 2 Peter 3:18. Add to this list any verses that encourage you in your spiritual and personal growth.

 Optional exercise–If you have *A Woman After God's Own Heart*™ *Prayer Journal*, just for today fill in the section titled "My Personal Growth" by writing out this statement and finishing it with words out of your own heart:

Lord, just for today, help me to grow in grace and knowledge by…

On the following page, relate in 100 words or less one instance when you actively chose to put a new discipline into practice. Then thank God for His grace to make that choice.

Heart Exercise 18

A Heart Enriched by Joy in the Lord

 In your personal copy of *A Woman After God's Own Heart*™ read chapter 18, "A Heart Enriched by Joy in the Lord." Make notes here about what meant the most to you from this chapter or offered you the greatest challenge or inspired you deeply.

In our previous exercise, we began an exciting journey of looking at God's pattern, plan, and desire for our spiritual and personal growth. Why grow? Note how a few scriptures answer this question.

Romans 8:29–

Ephesians 2:10–

2 Timothy 1:9–

2 Peter 1:5-8–

As I stated before, this section on "self" is about preparing your "self" for ministry so that your life overflows naturally in ministry into the lives of others. "Self" is the mainspring to ministry. Therefore, as women after God's own heart, we must do all that we can (our part) so that God can grow us into women who bless others through our encouragement, our instruction, our helps, our faith, our knowledge. On and on goes the list of ways we can minister to others. So let's spend some additional time considering several more facets of spiritual and personal growth.

♡ *Spiritual growth is aided by discipleship*–Please, just one more time, read Titus 2:3-5. What are the two categories of women named in these verses?

And what is the role of each?

Also, make a list of the four traits that distinguish a godly older woman.

1.

2.

3.

4.

Now list the curriculum these older women are to teach to the younger ones.

1.   5.

2.   6.

3.   7.

4.

And why, according to verse 5, was it important that these attitudes be passed on?

Who is your older woman, and who are your younger women? Name them here, and then read from my own interactions with Christian women.

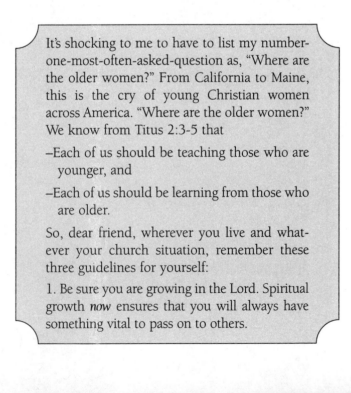

It's shocking to me to have to list my number-one-most-often-asked-question as, "Where are the older women?" From California to Maine, this is the cry of young Christian women across America. "Where are the older women?" We know from Titus 2:3-5 that

–Each of us should be teaching those who are younger, and

–Each of us should be learning from those who are older.

So, dear friend, wherever you live and whatever your church situation, remember these three guidelines for yourself:

1. Be sure you are growing in the Lord. Spiritual growth *now* ensures that you will always have something vital to pass on to others.

2. Don't give up in your search for an "older woman." There are numerous older women who have put their wisdom in writing. Good books abound that come from the hearts and souls and minds of a multitude of older women in the faith. Also try to attend events where older women are speaking and sharing their knowledge.

3. Realize that *you* may be one of the older women in your congregation. If so, don't resist. Embrace the reality and do all you can to serve those in your church.[17]

Spiritual growth is aided by goals–It's true that goals provide focus, specific measurement, and encouragement. Can you write out two or three spiritual growth goals for this next week? For instance, to have your quiet time each day. To read one chapter in a meaningful book. To memorize one verse of scripture. Now, write your own goals, commit them to God, and be sure and celebrate the progress made!

1.

2.

3.

Spiritual growth depends on choices–Everything is a choice. We choose to turn on the TV or to pick up a good book. We choose to talk on the phone or to work on a Bible study. We choose to go out to visit or shop or we choose to meet with an older woman. We choose to collapse during the baby's nap (and sometimes we need to do just that!) or to listen to a tape series or work on a correspondence course.

As you look at these examples and think about your own set of choices, do you see any patterns? Or, put another way, what choices are you consistently making? And are they the choices that lead you to spiritual growth? Take a few minutes to write out your observations. (This is an important exercise, so you may want to use an extra piece of paper or your prayer journal!)

Spiritual growth requires time–Read again #3 on pages 32-33 and the ending paragraph on page 34. Isn't this what we both want as women after God's own heart?! But it takes time...each day...for each year...for each decade. So, what will you do today to grow? And each day this next week? Giving these goals a timeframe will put you one week down the road toward an enriched heart and an enriched life. (By the way, this is a good exercise to repeat every week!)

Day 1   Day 5

Day 2   Day 6

Day 3   Day 7

Day 4

Spiritual growth results in ministry–"You cannot give away what you do not possess." We'll look more at your ministry in the next lesson, but realize for now that if you're faithful to grow, your life—by God's grace—*will* overflow in ministry to others.

💜 *Spiritual growth results in joy in the Lord*–Describe a woman you know whose life seems to overflow in joy as she shares her growth in the Lord with others. How does her joy show? How is it obvious? And what does her joy do for you as God enables her to share His joy with you and others?

And how does her spiritual joy motivate you to grow in the Lord?

Verses to memorize–Ephesians 2:10 and 2 Peter 1:8. Add to this list any verses that encourage you to grow in Christ.

Optional exercise–If you have *A Woman After God's Own Heart™ Prayer Journal*, just for today fill in the section titled "My Personal Growth" by writing out this statement and finishing it with words out of your own heart:

Lord, just for today, help me to grow by...

On the following page, relate in 100 words or less one instance when you actively chose to pursue spiritual growth before participating in some other activity. Then thank God for His grace to make that choice.

Words from My Heart

Heart Exercise 19

A Heart That Shows It Cares and Encourages Others

In your personal copy of *A Woman After God's Own Heart*™ read chapter 19, "A Heart That Shows It Cares." Make notes here about what meant the most to you from this chapter or offered you the greatest challenge or inspired you deeply.

💛 *Reflect on God's plan*–So far we've spent 18 chapters looking at God's Word and seeking to determine what His priorities are for us as women after His own heart. We know of God's command to love Him supremely (Luke 10:27). Beyond that we've culled through Titus 2:3-5 over and over again where the priorities of *husband*, *children*, and *home* are spelled out. And finally, we finished considering our *self*–the nurturing of our spiritual growth. And now we come to, by God's grace, the outpouring and the overflowing of all that's gone before–a life ready for rich ministry to others. Picture again the illustration of the Seven Sacred Pools on pages 194-196. How did this depiction of the natural order and overflow of your priorities help you to understand the flow of God's plan for you?

What adjustment or corrections do you need to make in order for this picture to become reality in your life?

Now that we've considered God's plan for our loved ones and the additional blessing we can be to others, let's look at ten ways we can influence the lives of others—countless others—for eternity.

1. *Learn to reach out*—Look at the aspects of giving or reaching out to others that are included in Luke 6:30-38. In a word, what is Jesus' command (verse 30)?

—What is the scope (verses 30 and 35)?

—What is to be expected (verses 30 and 35)?

—Who does God give to in verse 35?

—How much are we to give (verse 38)?

Now, write out any changes you need to make in your reaching out and giving to others.

2. *Learn to look out*—Take a quick look at Jesus' parable of "the Good Samaritan." List the variety of ways he "looked out" for the wounded man in Luke 10:25-37.

How did he manifest a "bountiful eye"?

And how was he direct when he saw a person in need?

What is your normal pattern when you go to church (or elsewhere)? Do you notice–even intentionally look for–those who are hurting or lost? Think this through and answer honestly. Then, once again, note any changes that you need to make.

3. *Go to give*–Which point (be all there, live to the hilt, or divide and conquer) meant the most to you in this section, and why?

Once again, are there changes you need to make in your ministry style and heart?

4. *Develop your prayer life*–Did "Will" get his point across to you–that prayer involves the "Will" and is "Willful"? So…when do you pray?

Where do you pray?

And what is your plan?

Now read chapter 20, "A Heart That Encourages." Make notes here about what meant the most to you from this chapter or offered you the greatest challenge or inspired you deeply. Then continue on with our list of ten ways we can, by God's good grace, influence the lives of others.

5. *Take time to be filled*–It's true that there are skills we can develop to strengthen our ministry. What would you consider to be a area of weakness in your life, one that tends to hinder you in the area of ministry to others?

Now list steps you can take this week to strengthen this weak area.

6. *Memorize scriptures of encouragement*–Hopefully you've been faithful to memorize the scriptures suggested each week. (And, when you've finished this growth and study guide, it will be fun to begin choosing your own verses!) Share an instance when you used one of your memorized scriptures from these lessons to encourage someone else.

7. *Make phone calls to encourage*–Who needs your call today? Determine not to withhold that sunshine call...when it's in the power of your hand to give it (Proverbs 3:27)!

8. *Write notes of encouragement*–And who needs your note of encouragement today? Again, don't withhold! Do it! Write it! Right now!

9. *Encourage others through three spiritual gifts*–I was thrilled to discover these three ministries that all Christians can have and use in the body of Christ. Read Romans 12:7-8 and then answer these questions:

Who can you *serve* today and how? (Yes, your husband and children count–indeed, they have top priority! Can you also think of others?)

Who needs your *mercy*?

And how and to whom can you *give*?

Now be faithful to follow through on the thoughts God brought to your mind!

10. *Live your priorities*–As you have begun to live out God's priorities in your life and in your family, what remarks have people made concerning the differences and changes in your life?

Do you agree that living out your priorities and modeling God's plan ministers to many? Explain, please.

 Verses to memorize—Proverbs 3:27 and 1 Corinthians 15:58. Add to this list any verses that encourage you in your ministry.

 Optional exercise—If you have *A Woman After God's Own Heart™ Prayer Journal*, just for today fill in the section titled "My Ministry" by writing out this statement and finishing it with words out of your own heart:

Lord, just for today, help me to reach out and encourage [insert a name here] _____ by...

On the following page, relate in 100 words or less one instance when you actively chose to reach out and encourage someone. Then thank God for His grace to make that choice.

THE PRACTICE
OF GOD'S PRIORITIES

THE PRACTICE OF GOD'S PRIORITIES

Heart Exercise 20

A Heart That Seeks God First and Follows Him

In your personal copy of *A Woman After God's Own Heart*™ read chapter 21, "A Heart That Seeks First Things First." Make notes here about what meant the most to you from this chapter or offered you the greatest challenge or inspired you deeply.

💟 *A word about priorities*—Did the little poem on pages 217-218 describe you, my friend? How many hats do you feel like you're trying to wear at once? List them here. Which ones seem to be the most demanding and why?

💟 *A word about choices*—Read these quotes from your book and mark the one you like the best or that motivates you the most and tell why:

128

- As now, so then.
- What you are today is what you are becoming.
- You are today what you have been becoming.
- (And an extra...) Each day is a little life, and our whole life is but a day repeated.

♡ *A word about others*–List the "others" (people, positions, and pastimes) in your life. Our priorities certainly don't end with the number 6! Pray first, and then try to put them in an order that honors God and reflects His values. (And don't forget to ask your husband to help you prioritize! His insights and perspectives will reveal what he is observing and thinking.)

♡ *A word about waiting*–How are you when it comes to waiting? Do you tend to be a person who operates on impulse, makes spur-of-the-moment decisions, and swings and sways from opportunity to option? Or are you a woman who is patient, who prays, who prioritizes, and who plans? Can you give an example?

♡ *Some women who adjusted their priorities*–We looked at several other women in this chapter. Now, how would *your* story read? Do you think your priorities are in order? Does your husband think so? And how about your children? Be honest. And be brave enough to make some serious changes.

Now read chapter 22, "Following After God's Heart." Make notes here about what meant the most to you from this chapter or offered you the greatest challenge or inspired you deeply.

1. *Plan your day*—Two sayings immediately come to my mind here!

> • If you don't plan your day, someone else will be happy to plan it for you.
>
> • God has a wonderful plan for your life...and so does everyone else!

Planning is a good first step toward practicing your priorities. So stop and plan whatever is left of your day today. Then, before you go to bed tonight, jot down those events that are already set for tomorrow—mealtimes, appointments, responsibilities. That's a good beginning on tomorrow's wonderful day.

2. *Pray over your plans and priorities*—Continuing on with the exercise you began above (or the evening before), and using the list of your priorities from pages 229-231, pray your way through your plan, writing out your planned activities. If you have the *A Woman After God's Own Heart*™ *Prayer Journal*, write your plans for practicing your priorities there under the appropriate sections—God, husband, children, etc.

3. *Schedule your plans and priorities*–If planning is the *what* of your day, scheduling is the *how*. On your calendar or day-planner write down *when* you intend to follow through on each of the plans. If you're unsure how to do this, look again at the examples.

4. *Practice your priorities*–Now it's time to live out your plan and practice your priorities. Just for one day, think in terms of the numbers assigned to your priorities on page 233 (#1=God; #2=husband; #3=children; #4=home; #5=self; #6=ministry; #7=others). I think you'll find this numbers exercise helpful, practical, and very eye-opening!

5. *Acquire God's perspective on your day*–Do you share my friend's perspective on your days? She definitely had honoring the Lord with each and every day in mind when she wrote...

> To treat each day as if it and it *alone* were our "golden day"–then what a beautiful string of golden days becoming golden years we would have to give back to our Lord!

This perspective, dear friend, is the *how* of practicing our priorities, and it's also the *why*. What changes in your perspective or attitude toward each new day do you need to make to acquire this worthy perspective?

6. *Practice, practice, practice!*–How do you and I become women after God's own heart? By practice, practice, practice! By practicing our priorities one day at a time...for the

rest of our lives. By living our lives God's way, according to God's Word. By spending our precious time, energy, and days in the pursuit of God's best. Purpose to practice...just for today, your "golden day."

 Verses to memorize–Deuteronomy 33:25b and Matthew 6:33. Add to this list any verses that encourage you on your journey toward becoming a woman after God's own heart.

 Optional exercise–If you have *A Woman After God's Own Heart*™ *Prayer Journal*, just for today fill in the section titled "My Heart Response" by writing out this statement and finishing it with words out of your own heart:

Lord, just for today, help me to live out this one golden day by...

On the following page, relate in 100 words or less one instance when you actively chose to practice your priorities. Then thank God for His grace to make that choice.

Words from My Heart

From My Heart
To Yours

If you'll remember, I mentioned in the beginning of my book that you and I were embarking on a journey–a journey of learning about God's priorities and how to practice them, a journey of discovering and implementing the disciplines that mark us out as women after God's own heart, a journey toward greater growth and ministry to others.

Well, you've obviously taken the first steps by reading the book *A Woman After God's Own Heart™*...and now you've taken additional steps by working through this growth and study guide to becoming a woman after God's own heart. You've definitely come a long way already, and I'm certain you're experiencing a transformed life just by your obedience to practice God's priorities for your life.

And now, dear one, as we part and continue down our paths of pursuing Him and His good, better, and best, may God give you His grace, mercy, and peace on your journey to becoming a woman after God's own heart. May He continually bring His truths and His principles to your mind. May He reveal fresh, new ways for you to follow after Him. May the evidence of your growth and your walk with the Lord sound forth the Word of the Lord (1 Thessalonians 1:8) for all to hear and behold. May your loved ones be blessed. And may you stand tall alongside the Proverbs 31 woman. May it be said of you, too, "Many daughters have done well, but you excel them all" (Proverbs 31:29).

In His exceedingly great and precious love,

Elizabeth

Heart Exercise 1–

What are some of the things that keep you from having a daily quiet time?

What do you think are the key ingredients to a quality quiet time?

Heart Exercise 2–

What could you give up in order to spend time in God's Word?

How should a deep conviction about the benefits, power, and importance of time in God's Word affect us?

Heart Exercise 3–

As a group, compile and share a list of helpful hints for finding time for prayer.

As a group, compile and share a list of ideas for an exciting time of prayer. (For instance, begin your time of prayer by reading one psalm.)

Heart Exercise 4–

Make up an acrostic for the word **O-B-E-Y**.

See if you can add to the list of the benefits of obedience.

Heart Exercise 5–

What are some ways you have helped your husband this past week?

How can Philippians 2:3-4 apply to you as a wife in this area of serving your husband?

Heart Exercise 6–

What is or has been the greatest struggle for you in the area of submission?

How have you seen God honor your obedience when you have submitted?

Heart Exercise 7–

How do you make your husband feel special? Be specific.

Share how God answered one of your prayers for your husband this past week.

Heart Exercise 8–

What do you do to prepare yourself for your husband's homecoming each evening (mentally, physically, and spiri-tually)?

What strengths do you see in your husband? Have you ever told him you are aware of these strengths and appreciate them?

Heart Exercise 9–

What are some materials or exercises you have used with your children to teach them God's Word and wisdom?

What time of day works best for you and your family for focusing on God's Word, and why?

Heart Exercise 10–

What are the top three prayer requests you pray for your children?

How can a "little" excuse today affect your children in a "big" way tomorrow?

Heart Exercise 11–

How would you describe the general emotional tone of your home?

Which one of the five marks of motherly affection, if applied, would make the biggest difference in the general emotional tone of your home?

Heart Exercise 12–

As you worked your way through the section on mothering, how is your view of your role as a mother changing?

Which one of the additional five marks of motherly affection, if applied, would make the biggest difference in the general emotional tone of your home?

Heart Exercise 13–

Share a time when you knew your home environment min-istered to someone else.

Share a time when the home environment of someone else ministered to you.

Heart Exercise 14-

What are the things that tend to rob you of time from watching over your home?

How–and what–are you teaching your children about the value of hardwork?

Heart Exercise 15-

Describe your week and the difference the 12 "little steps" in time management made in creating order from chaos.

What favorite time management tip or resources can you recommend to the group?

Heart Exercise 16-

As you think about this section on the home, what new atti-tudes and/or disciplines have you put into practice?

Share a challenging "I will"–either from page 169 or from your own list–with your group.

Heart Exercise 17-

Describe an encounter you've had with a "There you are!" person.

What do you think makes someone a "There you are!" person?

Heart Exercise 18-

Describe a time when you had the opportunity to learn from an older woman.

What are some things you're learning that are causing your life to overflow with joy?

Heart Exercise 19-

Share an opportunity you had this week to reach out to someone in need.

Share an opportunity you passed up this week to reach out to someone in need.

Heart Exercise 20-

How does the saying, "What you are today is what you are becoming" describe you?

What motivates you each new day to keep practicing your priorities?

LEADING A BIBLE STUDY DISCUSSION GROUP

What a privilege it is to lead a Bible study! And what joy and excitement await you as you delve into the Word of God and help others to discover its life-changing truths. If God has called you to lead a Bible study group, I know you'll be spending much time in prayer and planning and giving much thought to being an effective leader. I also know that taking the time to read through the following tips will help you to navigate the challenges of leading a Bible study discussion group and enjoying the effort and opportunity.

The Leader's Roles

As a Bible study group leader, you'll find your role changing back and forth from *expert* to *cheerleader* to *lover* to *referee* during the course of a session.

Since you're the leader, group members will look to you to be the *expert* guiding them through the material. So be well prepared. In fact, be overprepared so that you know the material better than any group member does. Start your study early in the week, and let its message simmer all week long. (You might even work several lessons ahead so that you have in mind the big picture and the overall direction of the study.) Be ready to share some additional gems that your group members wouldn't have discovered on their own. That extra insight from your study time—or that comment from a wise Bible teacher or scholar, that clever saying, that keen observation from another believer, and even an appropriate joke—adds an element of fun and keeps Bible study from becoming routine, monotonous, and dry.

Second, be ready to be the group's *cheerleader*. Your energy and enthusiasm for the task at hand can be contagious. It can also stimulate people to get more involved in their personal study as well as in the group discussion.

Third, be the *lover,* the one who shows a genuine concern for the members of the group. You're the one who will establish the atmosphere of the group. If you laugh and have fun, the group members will laugh and have fun. If you hug, they will hug. If you care, they will care. If you share, they will share. If you love, they will love. So pray every day to love the women God has placed in your group. Ask Him to show you how to love them with His love.

Finally, as the leader, you'll need to be the *referee* on occasion. That means making sure everyone has an equal opportunity to speak. That's easier to do when you operate under the assumption that every member of the group has something worthwhile to contribute. So, trusting that the Lord has taught each person during the week, act on that assumption.

Expert, cheerleader, lover, and referee—these four roles of the leader may make the task seem overwhelming. But that's not bad if it keeps you on your knees praying for your group.

A Good Start

Beginning on time, greeting people warmly, and opening in prayer gets the study off to a good start. Know what you want to have happen during your time together and make sure those things get done. That kind of order means comfort for those involved.

Establish a format and let the group members know what that format is. People appreciate being in a Bible study that focuses on the Bible. So keep the discussion on the topic and move the group through the questions. Tangents are often hard to avoid—and even harder to rein in. So be sure to focus on the answers to questions about the specific passage at hand. After all, the purpose of the group is Bible study!

Finally, as someone has accurately observed, "Personal growth is one of the by-products of any effective small group. This growth is achieved when people are recognized and accepted by others. The more friendliness, mutual trust, respect, and warmth exhibited, the more likely that the member will find pleasure in the group, and, too, the more likely she will work hard toward the accomplishment of the group's goals. The effective leader will strive to reinforce desirable traits" (source unknown).

A Dozen Helpful Tips

Here is a list of helpful suggestions for leading a Bible study discussion group:

1. Arrive early, ready to focus fully on others and give of yourself. If you have to do any last-minute preparation, review, re-grouping, or praying, do it in the car. Don't dash in, breathless, harried, late, still tweaking your plans.

2. Check out your meeting place in advance. Do you have everything you need—tables, enough chairs, a blackboard, hymnals if you plan to sing, coffee, etc.?

3. Greet each person warmly by name as she arrives. After all, you've been praying for these women all week long, so let each VIP know that you're glad she's arrived.

4. Use name tags for at least the first two or three weeks.

5. Start on time no matter what—even if only one person is there!

6. Develop a pleasant but firm opening statement. You might say, "This lesson was great! Let's get started so we can enjoy all of it!" or "Let's pray before we begin our lesson."

7. Read the questions, but don't hesitate to reword them on occasion. Rather than reading an entire paragraph of instructions, for instance, you might say, "Question 1 asks us to list some ways that Christ displayed humility. Lisa, please share one way Christ displayed humility."

8. Summarize or paraphrase the answers given. Doing so will keep the discussion focused on the topic; eliminate digressions; help avoid or clear up any misunderstandings of the

text; and keep each group member aware of what the others are saying.

9. Keep moving and don't add any of your own questions to the discussion time. It's important to get through the study guide questions. So if a cut-and-dried answer is called for, you don't need to comment with anything other than a "thank you." But when the question asks for an opinion or an application (for instance, "How can this truth help us in our marriages?" or "How do *you* find time for your quiet time?"), let all who want to contribute.

10. Affirm each person who contributes, especially if the contribution was very personal, painful to share, or a quiet person's rare statement. Make everyone who shares a hero by saying something like, "Thank you for sharing that insight from your own life" or, "We certainly appreciate what God has taught you. Thank you for letting us in on it."

11. Watch your watch, put a clock right in front of you, or consider using a timer. Pace the discussion so that you meet your cutoff time, especially if you want time to pray. Stop at the designated time even if you haven't finished the lesson. Remember that everyone has worked through the study once; you are simply going over it again.

12. End on time. You can only make friends with your group members by ending on time or even a little early! Besides, members of your group have the next item on their agenda to attend to—picking up children from the nursery, babysitter, or school; heading home to tend to matters there; running errands; getting to bed; or spending some time with their husbands. So let them out *on time!*

Five Common Problems

In any group, you can anticipate certain problems. Here are some common ones that can arise, along with helpful solutions:

1. *The incomplete lesson*—Right from the start, establish the policy that if someone has not done the lesson, it is best for her not to answer the questions. But do try to include her responses to questions that ask for opinions or experiences. Everyone can share some thoughts in reply to a question like, "Reflect on what you know about both athletic and spiritual training and then share what you consider to be the essential elements of training oneself in godliness."

2. *The gossip*—The Bible clearly states that gossiping is wrong, so you don't want to allow it in your group. Set a high and strict standard by saying, "I am not comfortable with this conversation," or "We [not *you*] are gossiping, ladies. Let's move on."

3. *The talkative member*—Here are three scenarios and some possible solutions for each.

   a. The problem talker may be talking because she has done her homework and is excited about something she has to share. She may also know more about the subject than the others and, if you cut her off, the rest of the group may suffer.

   SOLUTION: Respond with a comment like: "Sarah, you are making very valuable contributions. Let's see if we can get some reactions from the others," or "I know Sarah can answer this. She's really done her homework. How about some of the rest of you?"

   b. The talkative member may be talking because she has *not* done her homework and wants to contribute, but she has no boundaries.

   SOLUTION: Establish at the first meeting that those who have not done the lesson do not contribute except on opinion or application questions. You may need to repeat this guideline at the beginning of each session.

c. The talkative member may want to be heard whether or not she has anything worthwhile to contribute.

SOLUTION: After subtle reminders, be more direct, saying, "Betty, I know you would like to share your ideas, but let's give others a chance. I'll call on you later."

4. *The quiet member*—Here are two scenarios and possible solutions.

a. The quiet member wants the floor but somehow can't get the chance to share.

SOLUTION: Clear the path for the quiet member by first watching for clues that she wants to speak (moving to the edge of her seat, looking as if she wants to speak, perhaps even starting to say something) and then saying, "Just a second. I think Chris wants to say something." Then, of course, make her a hero!

b. The quiet member simply doesn't want the floor.

SOLUTION: "Chris, what answer do you have on question 2?" or "Chris, what do you think about…?" Usually after a shy person has contributed a few times, she will become more confident and more ready to share. Your role is to provide an opportunity where there is *no* risk of a wrong answer. But occasionally a group member will tell you that she would rather not be called on. Honor her request, but from time to time ask her privately if she feels ready to contribute to the group discussions.

In fact, give all your group members the right to pass. During your first meeting, explain that any time a group member does not care to share an answer, she may simply say, "I pass." You'll want to repeat this policy at the beginning of every group session.

5. *The wrong answer*—Never tell a group member that she has given a wrong answer, but at the same time never let a wrong answer go by.

SOLUTION: Either ask if someone else has a different answer or ask additional questions that will cause the right answer to emerge. As the women get closer to the right answer, say, "We're getting warmer! Keep thinking! We're almost there!"

Learning from Experience

Immediately after each Bible study session, evaluate the group discussion time. You may also want a member of your group (or an assistant or trainee or outside observer) to evaluate you periodically.

1. Elizabeth George, *A Woman After God's Own Heart* ™ (Eugene, OR: Harvest House Publishers, 1997).

2. Warren Wiersbe, ed., *The Best of A. W. Tozer* (Grand Rapids, MI: Baker Book House, 1978), pp. 149-51.

3. Elizabeth George, *A Woman After God's Own Heart*™ *Prayer Journal* (Eugene, OR: Harvest House Publishers, 1999).

4. C. A. Stoddards, source unknown.

5. John MacArthur, *The MacArthur Study Bible* (Nashville: Word Publishing, 1997), p. 1087.

6. Ibid., p. 1933.

7. Neil S. Wilson, ed., *The Handbook of Bible Application* (Wheaton, IL: Tyndale House Publishers, Inc., 1992), p. 441.

8. Ibid., pp. 441-43.

9. MacArthur, *The MacArthur Study Bible,* p. 19.

10. Charles F. Pfeiffer and Everett F. Harrison, eds., *The Wycliffe Bible Commentary* (Chicago: Moody Press, 1973), p. 5.

11. Mary Louise Kitsen,"Generations of Excuses," *Good News Broadcaster*, issue unknown, pp. 34-35.

12. Eleanor L. Doan, *The Speaker's Sourcebook*, quoting Mary Holmes from *The War Cry* (Grand Rapids, MI: Zondervan Publishing House, 1977), p. 27.

13. Sid Buzzell, gen. ed., *The Leadership Bible* (Grand Rapids, MI: Zondervan Publishing House, 1998), p. 739.

14. Doan, *The Speaker's Sourcebook*, quote by Christine Warren, p. 266.

15. Stoddards.

16. Author unknown, cited in Elizabeth George, *Beautiful in God's Eyes–The Treasures of the Proverbs 31 Woman*, (Eugene, OR: Harvest House Publishers, 1998), p. 210.

17. "Ask Elizabeth" at www.elizabethgeorge.com.

QUIET TIMES CALENDAR

Jan.	Feb.	Mar.	Apr.	May	June
1	1	1	1	1	1
2	2	2	2	2	2
3	3	3	3	3	3
4	4	4	4	4	4
5	5	5	5	5	5
6	6	6	6	6	6
7	7	7	7	7	7
8	8	8	8	8	8
9	9	9	9	9	9
10	10	10	10	10	10
11	11	11	11	11	11
12	12	12	12	12	12
13	13	13	13	13	13
14	14	14	14	14	14
15	15	15	15	15	15
16	16	16	16	16	16
17	17	17	17	17	17
18	18	18	18	18	18
19	19	19	19	19	19
20	20	20	20	20	20
21	21	21	21	21	21
22	22	22	22	22	22
23	23	23	23	23	23
24	24	24	24	24	24
25	25	25	25	25	25
26	26	26	26	26	26
27	27	27	27	27	27
28	28	28	28	28	28
29		29	29	29	29
30		30	30	30	30
31		31		31	

DATE BEGUN _____

July	Aug.	Sept.	Oct.	Nov.	Dec.
1	1	1	1	1	1
2	2	2	2	2	2
3	3	3	3	3	3
4	4	4	4	4	4
5	5	5	5	5	5
6	6	6	6	6	6
7	7	7	7	7	7
8	8	8	8	8	8
9	9	9	9	9	9
10	10	10	10	10	10
11	11	11	11	11	11
12	12	12	12	12	12
13	13	13	13	13	13
14	14	14	14	14	14
15	15	15	15	15	15
16	16	16	16	16	16
17	17	17	17	17	17
18	18	18	18	18	18
19	19	19	19	19	19
20	20	20	20	20	20
21	21	21	21	21	21
22	22	22	22	22	22
23	23	23	23	23	23
24	24	24	24	24	24
25	25	25	25	25	25
26	26	26	26	26	26
27	27	27	27	27	27
28	28	28	28	28	28
29	29	29	29	29	29
30	30	30	30	30	30
31	31		31		31

Personal Notes

Personal Notes

Personal Notes

Personal Notes

Personal Notes

Personal Notes

Personal Notes

Personal Notes

Personal Notes

Personal Notes

A Woman After God's Own Heart® Study Series

Bible Studies for Busy Women

God wrote the Bible to change hearts and lives. Every study in this series is written with that in mind—and is especially focused on helping Christian women know how God desires for them to live."

—Elizabeth George

Sharing wisdom gleaned from more than 20 years as a women's Bible study teacher, Elizabeth has prepared insightful lessons that can be completed in 15 to 20 minutes per day. Each lesson includes thought-provoking questions, insights, Bible study tips, instructions for leading a discussion group, and a "heart response" section to make the Bible passage more personal.

HARVEST HOUSE
PUBLISHERS
EUGENE, OREGON 97402
www.harvesthousepublishers.com

About the Author

Elizabeth George is a bestselling author and speaker whose passion is to teach the Bible in a way that changes women's lives. For information about Elizabeth's books or speaking ministry, to sign up for her mailings, or to share how God has used this book in your life, please write to Elizabeth at:

Elizabeth George
P.O. Box 2879
Belfair, WA 98528

Toll-free fax/phone: 1-800-542-4611
www.ElizabethGeorge.com

∾

Books by Elizabeth George

- Beautiful in God's Eyes
- Life Management for Busy Women
- Loving God with All Your Mind
- A Mom After God's Own Heart
- Powerful Promises for Every Woman
- The Remarkable Women of the Bible
- Small Changes for a Better Life
- A Wife After God's Own Heart
- A Woman After God's Own Heart®
- A Woman After God's Own Heart® Deluxe Edition
- A Woman's Call to Prayer
- A Woman's High Calling
- A Woman's Walk with God
- A Young Woman After God's Own Heart
- A Young Woman's Call to Prayer
- A Young Woman's Walk with God

Children's Books

- God's Wisdom for Little Girls

Study Guides

- Beautiful in God's Eyes Growth & Study Guide
- Life Management for Busy Women Growth & Study Guide
- Loving God with All Your Mind Growth & Study Guide
- A Mom After God's Own Heart Growth & Study Guide
- Powerful Promises for Every Woman Growth & Study Guide
- The Remarkable Women of the Bible Growth & Study Guide
- Small Changes for a Better Life Growth & Study Guide
- A Wife After God's Own Heart Growth & Study Guide
- A Woman After God's Own Heart® Growth & Study Guide
- A Woman's Call to Prayer Growth & Study Guide
- A Woman's High Calling Growth & Study Guide
- A Woman's Walk with God Growth & Study Guide

Books by Jim & Elizabeth George

- God Loves His Precious Children
- God's Wisdom for Little Boys

Books by Jim George

- God's Man of Influence
- A Husband After God's Own Heart
- A Man After God's Own Heart
- The Remarkable Prayers of the Bible
- The Remarkable Prayers of the Bible Growth & Study Guide
- A Young Man After God's Own Heart